# The *Good Guys* of
# BASEBALL

## Seventeen True Sports Stories

*by*
*Terry Egan, Stan Friedmann, and Mike Levine*

**ALADDIN PAPERBACKS**

New York   London   Toronto   Sydney   Singapore

First Aladdin Paperbacks edition March 2000

Aladdin Paperbacks
An imprint of Simon & Schuster
Children's Publishing Division
1230 Avenue of the Americas
New York, NY 10020

Designed by Corinne Allen
The text for this book was set in 13-point Goudy.
Printed and bound in the United States of America
2 4 6 8 10 9 7 5 3 1

The Library of Congress has cataloged the
hardcover edition as follows:
Egan, Terry, 1957–
The good guys of baseball / by Terry Egan, Stan Friedmann,
and Mike Levine. — 1st ed.
p. cm. Includes index.
Summary: A collection of inspirational stories about contemporary baseball
heroes, including Kirby Puckett, Ken Griffey, Jr.,
Cal Ripken, Jr., Jim Abbott, and Frank Thomas.
ISBN 0-689-80212-9 (hc.)
1. Baseball players–United States–Biography–Juvenile literature. 2. Baseball
players–United States–Conduct of life–Juvenile literature.
[1. Baseball players. 2. Conduct of Life.]
1. Friedmann, Stan. II. Levine, Mike. III. Title.
GV865.A1E33 1997 96-8512
ISBN 0-689-83318-0 (pbk.)

To our children—
Ben, Sam, Sunshine, Starlite, William,
Paul, Matthew, Sara,
Terry, Joe, Luke,
and the children of The Birch Family Camp

# ACKNOWLEDGMENTS

This book about Good Guys comes to you because the following good people stepped up to the plate and delivered. We thank them for their special contributions.

To Jennifer Flannery, who loves books and baseball.

To those who helped make crucial connections. . . . Suzyn Waldman, sportscaster at WFAN in New York City, Fran Freedman, who shares our vision, and Harold Underdown, who taught us the ropes.

To Linda Seligson, for understanding, for working long hours at the computer, and for sharing her love of the game with the kids.

To Cathie Egan, who knows about love and gets baseball.

To Regal Levine, for her endless devotion and eternal inspiration.

To Lou Zaklin, former Pirates scout, for his inspiration.

To our friends at the *Middletown Times Herald-Record*, and to Bill Kennedy, publisher of *The New Bedford Standard Times*, who, years ago, taught us how to tell a story.

# CONTENTS

# INTRODUCTION

*Grumble. Grumble, grumble. Grumble, grumble, grumble.*

That's the sound of older baseball fans talking about today's players. Some grown-ups say our national pastime is ruined. They say the modern ballplayer is selfish, lazy, and greedy. Young people have no role models to admire, they complain.

Welcome to *The Good Guys of Baseball*. Through these true stories we aim to prove those grumpy grumblers dead wrong. We're not saying the big leaguers in this book are perfect. They are decent human beings who have tried to do the right thing under pressure. Through their courage, hard work, and determination, they have given us a new generation of heroes to look up to. Of course the people in these stories are not the only good guys in baseball. There are countless good guys and women, in the big leagues and in your community. It's Mom or Dad playing catch with you even when they're tired from a hard day's work. It's a Little League coach who pats you on the back after you strike out with the bases loaded. And if you shrug off failure, cheer on your teammate who's up next, and hustle the rest of the game, you're a baseball hero, too.

This book is for you and the hero inside us all.

# The *Good Guys* of
# BASEBALL

# THE GIFT
## Mark McGwire and Sammy Sosa

*Boom. And there it goes. Wow, look at that rocket soar. That ball is disappearing deep into the center-field bleachers. Number 52 for muscle man Mark McGwire . . . Here's the windup and the pitch. Bang. Sammy Sosa's hit another one. Over the Wrigley Field wall, across the street onto Waveland Avenue. He rounds third base, touches his heart, and blows a kiss to his mom back home in the Dominican Republic . . . Blastoff. McGwire launches another one. He's bearing down on Roger Maris's mark of 61. Wait, we've just gotten word that Sosa's hit two home runs in Chicago. What a race they've got going!*

Boom, bang, blastoff. Welcome to the summer of 1998, with fireworks brought to you by Mark McGwire and Sammy Sosa. Every golden afternoon and every moonlit evening bring on the power parade of baseball's mightiest sluggers. Will they break the single-season home-run record set by the Yankees' Roger Maris way back in 1961?

It's all come down to this electric September

night in St. Louis, home of the Cardinals. Seems the whole world is watching Big Mac step up to the plate. They're watching in Sosa's hometown of San Pedro de Macoris, in Tokyo and Taiwan, in old farmhouses and Chicago high-rises. They're shouting here in St. Louis, in the stands at Busch Stadium, in the box seats where Roger Maris's family is cheering on McGwire, in the dugouts where players and coaches from both teams sit on edge.

And in right field, Sammy Sosa, who has chased Maris and McGwire all season long, is crouched with hands on knees, waiting, ready to pounce on anything hit his way.

All is still. Kids stop cracking peanuts. Beefy vendors put down their steaming cases of hot dogs and stare at the big man with the coiled bat.

The crowd builds to a roar and holds its breath, waiting to explode. The Chicago pitcher looks in for the sign. He may be holding baseball history in the palm of his hand.

McGwire cocks his bat, ready to deliver the present everyone's been waiting for. What wonderful gifts McGwire and Sosa have given baseball fans already! The monster home runs have everyone buzzing, sure. The race for the record has great-grandfathers talking to great-grandchildren about the fun-loving Babe Ruth and his 60 home runs in 1927. They get fathers talking to their kids about quiet Roger Maris, who broke the Babe's record.

But it's more than the home-run chase that has everyone talking. It's who McGwire and Sosa are, and the way they make everyone love baseball.

All season long, they've both been wonderful to the fans, giving high fives and kind words to thousands of kids across America. They've been neck and neck all summer, matching each other homer for homer. They've taken turns grabbing the lead in the chase to break the record.

They're coming down to the finish line together. Game by game, night after night, shot for shot, their names mentioned in the same breath. But the amazing thing is they started out from very different places.

The journey of Mark McGwire began in a nice suburban town in southern California. He had everything a young ballplayer needed—warm weather, the best equipment, and, oh, yes, lots of muscles. His parents were always there for him.

Mark was a big, strong kid, and the first time he got up to bat in a youth league, he hit the ball out of the park.

But as powerful as he looked, Mark was also shy. And the more the spotlight shone on him, the quieter he became. He took comfort in the shelter of hard work. If he was busy, no one would notice how shy he was. And, boy, did his hard work pay off. He became a high-school slugger, the *Sporting News* college player of the year, and a star for the 1984 U.S. Olympic silver-medal team.

When he made it to the major leagues in 1986 with the Oakland Athletics, he was ready for greatness. In his rookie season, McGwire belted 49 home runs, tops in the American League. He might have hit his fiftieth on the last day of the season, but something more important was happening. He joined his wife for the birth of their first child.

If Mark McGwire had almost everything going for him, young Sammy Sosa had almost nothing. Sammy grew up in San Pedro de Macoris, a poor town in the Dominican Republic where boys play baseball from sunup to sundown in hopes of a better life. But Sammy was so poor, he had no time to play ball. His father died when he was seven. His mother worked as a maid to support Sammy and his six brothers and sisters.

But Sammy felt rich from his mother's love. One time, he had no money for a Mother's Day gift, so he shined shoes. For all his hard work, he didn't earn enough to buy her a gift. So he gave his mother a kiss instead.

The first time he played baseball, he had to use a garbage bag for a glove. But the smart Dominican baseball coaches noticed something in Sosa that money couldn't buy—a real love for the game. No matter how hard he practiced, he always played for fun.

Sosa's journey to the majors was rockier than McGwire's. In order to make a better life for his family, he had to leave them and his country behind. He came to the United States to play minor league ball. He was alone in a new land. He didn't speak English; he wasn't used to American food. He felt like a stranger.

He arrived in the major leagues with the Texas Rangers, but he was quickly traded to the Chicago White Sox. He finished the season with only four home runs.

His arm was strong and he could throw out runners easily. Sometimes he would play great, but other times he would throw wildly, and strike out three times in a game. The fans called him Sammy So-So.

In 1991, he was even sent down to the minor leagues for a while. He felt like a yo-yo. When he came back up to the White Sox, he barely hit .200 and he struck out nearly one hundred times. As much as he loved his new country, he missed the place where he grew up. And even he began to wonder about his future in baseball. Then he was traded to the Cubbies. It was the same town, but a new league and a fresh start.

The Cubs fans adopted him right away. They loved his great arm, great hustle, and great swing. And even when he struck out, they stuck with him.

His first full year with the Cubs, he banged 33 round-trippers. He kept the fans in the bleachers supplied with free baseballs as he tattooed home runs over the ivy-covered brick wall. Sometimes he hit the ball so far it went clear out of the ballpark and landed across the street.

Back in the American League, McGwire kept banging home runs, too, but something was wrong. He and his wife got a divorce, and he felt sad. He missed his son.

The big guy became even more shy. He'd round the bases after a home run, looking like he couldn't wait to get back to the dugout. Even when his team won the World Series in 1989 and they were all celebrating, McGwire stayed in the background.

In 1991, McGwire batted only .201, among the worst averages in the league. He felt all mixed-up. He wanted to straighten out his life.

All the work he had put into baseball he now put into working things out with himself and his family. He faced his problems. Little by little, he began to feel better, clearer. Things began to make sense. He and his ex-wife became friends again, even though they were no longer married. They worked together to make sure their son, Matthew, had time together with each of them. Mark spent a lot more time with his son, and they became close.

He felt like Mark McGwire again. As major league pitchers would find out, he was ready for true greatness.

McGwire and Sosa were both hitting their home-run stride in the 1997 season. McGwire was traded to the St. Louis Cardinals and, after a slow start, began bombing away. But nothing could have prepared either of them for what happened in 1998.

And so here we are on September 8 in St. Louis with millions of baseball fans around the world looking on. The mighty McGwire stands at the plate, bat cocked. The Cubs pitcher goes into his windup. The crowd holds its breath.

And here's the pitch.

McGwire swings. His bat sends the ball screaming on a straight line. It hurtles past the infield, into the outfield, toward the left-field foul pole. Will it stay fair? Will it be high enough to go over the fence?

It's gone!

Number 62 and Mark McGwire is the new single-season home-run king.

The crowd roars, but it's not the roar of competition. This is a happier sound, like kids coming down the stairs on Christmas morning.

McGwire pumps his arms in jubilation. He's so excited that when he rounds first he forgets to touch the base. He runs back and stomps on the bag. Then he continues toward second, slower now, almost floating around the bases.

The Cubs infielders—the guys on the other team—stop McGwire to shake his hand. Out in right field, Sammy Sosa quietly taps his glove in applause.

McGwire rounds third and heads for home. The Cubs catcher shakes his hand and as McGwire touches the plate, the slugger disappears into the cover of his mobbing teammates all the way back to the dugout. After all, he's always been shy and it's hard for him to receive all this attention.

But Mark McGwire has gifts to give. He emerges from his teammates' embrace and goes straight to the first row, where his son is sitting. He gives him a big hug.

Then he goes over to the Maris family. Roger had passed away fourteen years earlier, but McGwire wants to make certain the world remembers the quiet Yankee. The new home-run king hugs the Maris family. He pounds on his heart and points his hand to heaven in memory of Roger.

And then the crowd, which couldn't possibly seem to roar any louder, explodes. Sammy Sosa is coming in from right field, and McGwire picks up the Cub and gives him the biggest bear hug of all.

They cheer in St. Louis, Chicago, and San Pedro de Macoris. Baseball fans across the world smile. McGwire broke the record first, but this is a moment without a loser.

No one knew how many more gifts there would be. That McGwire would finish the season with a sensational 70 home runs and Sosa an amazing 66. That McGwire would give time and money to make sure children everywhere were not mistreated. That Sosa would spend his off-season helping out his countrymen and countrywomen who were battered by a terrible hurricane.

But for that moment, when McGwire and Sosa

embraced, no gift could be sweeter. That hug told the story of two sluggers who traveled very different roads, played on opposing teams, and raced for the same finish line. Because of their friendship, what started out as a two-man home-run race ended up being a party where everyone was invited.

And we all came together to celebrate the great season of joy.

# KING OF HEARTS

## Joe Ausanio

On an icy December morning, we set out to find the good guys of baseball. Our car huffed up the snow-covered Hudson Valley to the old city of Kingston, New York. We turned into a narrow country road searching for the home of fireballing Joe Ausanio, relief pitcher for the New York Yankees.

"He must be really rich," said young Ben, whose dad had allowed him to skip school for this special meeting. "I bet he lives in a huge mansion."

Instead, the road took us to a tiny yellow trailer. We checked the directions twice. This must be it.

We slid along the icy driveway and knocked on the door. Ben bounced up and down with excitement. He had never met a major leaguer before.

We heard hard footsteps coming closer. A husky guy opened the door and smiled. "Hiya," he said, extending his large right hand. "Glad you found me. Come on in."

Ben looked confused. The only time he had seen

Joe Ausanio, the big righty, was on the mound at Yankee Stadium striking out big-league hitters, tipping his cap to the cheers of forty thousand fans. The person who answered the door was an everyday man in jeans and a T-shirt.

We walked inside, looking for trophies and framed photos. All we saw was a daddy getting ready to feed his two boys. But first, he had to finish the last of his magic tricks.

"I promised," he explained.

Holding a deck of cards, Joe Ausanio had Ben pick one out. It was the king of hearts. Ausanio made it disappear.

"Hey, where is it?" asked Ben, his mouth opened in amazement.

"Right here," said Ausanio, making the king of hearts appear again.

"Wow!" Ben said. "How did you do that?"

Most tricksters simply respond that it's magic. Joe Ausanio answered, "Hard work. Here, I'll show you how it's done."

He revealed the secrets of the trick and then went to feed his boys a hot lunch. We asked Ausanio how he did it.

"What, the magic trick?" he asked. "I just showed you."

"No," we said. "Making it to the major leagues; it sounds like an incredible story."

Ausanio shrugged his shoulders. He seemed shy

*The Ausanio team sticks together.*

talking about himself. "I'm just glad I made it," he said. "I'm no big star."

"Please, Joe," we said. "Tell your story for the young fans. They hear all about it when a ballplayer does something bad. They deserve to know about the good guys of baseball."

"Okay," he said. "I'll tell it for the kids. Grab a seat, Ben."

As a cold wind rattled the trailer, Joe Ausanio began to tell a story we would never forget. Listen:

"Our family didn't have a lot of money. My dad

worked every job he could to keep food on the table. But we didn't care if we were rich—we had baseball.

"Every day after school the neighborhood kids played ball in an empty parking lot. Boy, that was great. I was a big Red Sox fan and I'd pretend to be the entire Boston lineup. I'd imitate Fred Lynn, Jim Rice, all those guys.

"I don't know how many windows we broke, but a home run was worth the trouble we got into. And Little League, I loved it. When I was ten, I hit one over the fence. . . . "

As Joe Ausanio began to unfold his story, he looked like he was ten years old again. He wore a proud boy's smile. Ben talked about Little League, too, and they traded stories. Ben couldn't believe he was hanging out with a real New York Yankee.

Then Joe told him there was more to reaching the major leagues than fun and a fastball. "It's harder than that," he said. "Kind of like growing up.

"In 1984, I was drafted by the Atlanta Braves out of Kingston High School. I wanted to be a major leaguer more than anything in the world. I was ready to sign.

"Then I talked with my dad. He said, 'Get an education, no one can ever take that away from you.' It was a tough choice."

Ausanio said no to pro ball. Instead, he went to college in Jacksonville, Florida. He worked toward a degree and played baseball for the school team.

All the players had been stars on their high school teams. "They were all good," said Joe. "Some of the guys crumbled because they weren't big shots anymore."

The Kingston kid just decided to be himself, work hard, and not worry how good anyone else was. He made lots of friends. Four years later, he was drafted by the Pittsburgh Pirates.

"It was a dream come true," said Ausanio. "I thought I'd be in the big leagues soon."

Ben could feel the excitement. He pictured himself being signed up by a real major-league team. "What was it like playing for the Pirates?" he asked Joe.

Ausanio chuckled as he put his boys' lunch dishes away. "Not so fast, Ben. You have to play in the minor leagues first until they think you're good enough."

In his first year in the minor leagues, he did great. Smokin' Joe Ausanio blew the ball by strong hitters, striking out at least one batter every inning. The next year, he led the entire league in saves and was voted the Pirates' Minor League Pitcher of the Year.

"Way to go, Joe," said Ben.

"Thanks," said Ausanio. "When the next season began, my dad came to Albany to see me pitch. That was real exciting."

On that special day, Joe thanked his father for giving him solid advice about going to college. He had made the right choice about school and his baseball career was soaring. "I know you'll make it," said his dad.

Three days later, on Easter Sunday, Joseph Ausanio Sr. died. Joe was crushed. He missed his dad a lot.

"I couldn't believe he wouldn't see me play anymore."

All Joe could do was dedicate himself to his dream, using the work ethic he had learned from his dad.

He led his team in saves that year. A baseball magazine chose him as the top relief-pitching prospect in the entire Pirates organization.

The Pirates invited Ausanio to their 1991 major-league spring-training camp. He was excited, and not just about baseball, either. His wife was expecting their first baby.

That spring, Ausanio threw five innings without allowing a run. But after two weeks, they demoted Ausanio to a low minor league.

They said he had to work on a new pitch to go along with his fastball and forkball. Ausanio didn't understand—he was getting hitters out.

"That wasn't fair," said Ben. Joe smiled.

"Ben, did you ever do something good at home or in school and no one noticed? That's what it was like. I was mad, but I couldn't quit just because it was unfair."

Ausanio kept working hard in the minor leagues. He made it up to the Buffalo Bisons, the Pirates' top minor-league team. "Things were looking up."

On July 8, his wife, Tammy, gave birth to Joseph Ausanio III. Ausanio's smile faded as he talked about what happened next.

Eight days after he was born, little Joe got real sick. Ausanio rushed home. The doctors told him his boy might die. He had an infection in his brain.

For the next five weeks, Joe stayed in the hospital room with his sick baby. "I would have given anything to trade places with him," said Ausanio. He refused to rejoin his team until little Joe felt better.

"I realized my baseball career wasn't important compared to my son's health."

Little Joe began to get better. But he was unable to hear. He might not ever be able to.

Big Joe tried to get back to baseball. The trouble was he walked around feeling dizzy. One time, he collapsed, gasping for breath.

The doctors couldn't figure out what was wrong. His baseball season was over, maybe his whole career. He had to get to the bottom of this.

Ausanio talked about his dizziness with friends and family and counselors. He came to understand that he was still upset about his dad dying and then when his son got sick, Joe felt very afraid for him. He still couldn't bear being away from his wife and son.

Joe understood that he had kept all his feelings

inside. After a while, they kind of bubbled over into dizziness. He was having something called panic attacks.

Ausanio's doctor found a safe medicine to help him, and Joe found a new way to relax — learning magic tricks. He didn't need the medicine anymore.

In 1992, Ausanio got back into baseball with the Bisons. He worked hard, perfecting his fastball and forkball, throwing day in and day out. He made a mental note of every pitch he threw to every batter.

Joe was having a great year for the Pirates' top minor-league club. To top it off, Pittsburgh's big-league club needed relief pitching badly.

After all the struggling, it looked like Joe's big moment had finally arrived. He waited for a call from the Pirates.

The call never came.

"No fair," said Ben.

"I really felt I could have helped them," said Ausanio.

In fact, the Pirates had no use for him at all. The Montreal Expos picked him up. Ausanio had a great minor-league season for them, but no luck. The Expos wanted to demote him the next year.

It looked like it was all over for Ausanio. But a Yankee scout who had once been with the Expos remembered Joe. "This guy is good," the scout told his boss. "Good stuff, good attitude. He's worth a shot."

The Yanks signed him to a minor-league contract.

Ausanio started off 1994 striking out every minor leaguer in sight. By July, the Yankees needed help in the bullpen. Once again, Ausanio waited for a call.

The Yanks called everyone but him.

Maybe his dream of getting to the major leagues wasn't meant to be, Ausanio thought to himself. Maybe he should concentrate on building a new career to support Tammy, Joe, and their new baby, Kevin.

Joe sat in a hotel room watching the 1994 All-Star game, seeing all the players he had hoped to pitch against. It was just a fantasy, like when he played ball as a kid and pretended he was a Red Sox slugger.

At 9 P.M. the phone rang. "Joe," said the voice. "Pack your bags, you're going to New York."

Joe Ausanio just held the phone in his hand. He was stunned.

He thought of his dad, wishing he could tell him the good news. He thought about how hard he had worked, how much his family had endured, and how much he loved them. He was so happy he cried.

"I knew it had all been worth it," Ausanio told Ben. "I had finally made it to the majors, and no one could take that away from me."

Joe quickly became one of the most popular players in the Yankee clubhouse. They decided he was a good guy, not stuck up. On the airplane rides, he delighted his teammates with his card tricks. "Wade Boggs really got a kick out of them."

The Yanks got a bigger kick when they saw Ausanio pitch.

"Do you have any videos of yourself?" asked Ben.

Ausanio searched for a tape and popped it into his VCR. "My mom recorded this," he said. Ausanio fast-forwarded the tape to his favorite spot.

There he was, on the pitcher's mound at Yankee Stadium. It was his first appearance there. "I was nervous," he confided to Ben. But he had practiced those pitches for so long, it didn't matter.

Watching the TV screen, Ben saw a tall strong man wave a menacing bat. It was Dave Winfield, future Hall of Famer. Ausanio went into his windup. "Here comes a fastball up and in," he told Ben. Winfield swung and missed and headed back to the dugout.

"Cool," said Ben.

Then he watched as Otis Nixon came up to bat. Nixon was a speedy contact hitter who hardly ever struck out. Ausanio threw a pitch that started out straight as an arrow. Nixon swung. But suddenly the ball swooped down into the dirt. Strike three.

"Wow, it's like magic the way that ball moves," said Ben. "Just like the king of hearts trick."

"No," said Ausanio, "it's all about hard work."

We saw Joe's little boys were starting to get restless. Dad picked them up in his strong arms. "Nap time," he said.

It was time for us to go. Ben thanked him and they shook hands. Joe signed a baseball for him. It said, "From one ballplayer to another."

When we got back into the car, Ben was smiling from ear to ear. "He's a good guy."

In time, major-league hitters figured out the trick to Joe Ausanio's forkball. They laid off it, and when his fastball came in, they were ready. They battered Joe all over the ballpark.

In the summer of 1995, Joe Ausanio was sent back to the minors. He stood alone in the Yankee clubhouse, packing his bags. "No excuses," he said. "I didn't get the job done."

He didn't quit, either. Ausanio worked his way back to the Yankees, and the Mets signed him later that year. He moved into a new house near Kingston and his kids grew big and strong. Little Joe received surgery to help him hear.

As you read this, we don't know if Joe Ausanio will be playing in the major leagues. He'll certainly never make it into the Baseball Hall of Fame. Few players do. But if they had a special building to honor the personal courage of an athlete, a father's devotion, and a man's determination, Joe Ausanio would be in there.

His plaque would read, "The King of Hearts."

# A MOTHER'S MESSAGE

## Kirby Puckett

Dare anyone who claims baseball isn't the great game it used to be. Stand up to the smart alecks who shout that today's ballplayers are only in it for the money. Challenge those old-timers who don't believe in your heroes.

Tell them to check out the one and only Kirby Puckett.

There's Kirby now, roaming center field, pounding his glove, daring Atlanta Braves slugger Ron Gant to belt one over his head. See the white ball rocket toward the distant fence. Kirby chases after it, his short thick legs churning like a cannonball on wheels, back, back, back to the black baggy wall.

"You can get it," Kirby hears a voice rise inside him. "You can catch this one." As the ball disappears the center fielder leaps. He's got it.

Now Puckett's bouncing back to the dugout under a shower of Minnesota applause. He's running with a little boy's smile, not a braggart's smirk, but full of honest-to-goodness pleasure at snaring a baseball out of thin air.

Hear the message in the children's cheers. This game lives on. For the same baseball gods of joy who sent Kirby his own childhood heroes—Ernie Banks and Willie Mays—have delivered us this two-hundred-pound tank of baseball magic.

Like most great feats of magic, Kirby Puckett's triumph seems beyond belief.

⚾ ⚾ ⚾

Look higher than a fly ball. See the roofs of the red-hot brick buildings bake in the sweltering sun. These are the Robert Taylor Houses, home to twenty thousand of Chicago's poorest people. Some lack for food; many more are short on hope.

Come down to the fourteenth floor, where a strong woman sits by an open window wishing for a breeze. See her looking down on the waiting night. She watches her son.

Down on the checkerboard pavement, a small boy in shorts, smaller than the rest, is racing to the rock that is second base. The shortstop's throw comes in. The boy slides on the hot asphalt. He's safe!

Kirby Puckett stands up in the twilight, knees skinned, face smiling. This is paradise. He and the boys have been playing their game with a broomstick and red rubber ball since right after breakfast.

As the sun goes down, he hears a familiar voice calling out from the fourteenth-floor window.

"Kirby," comes the call. "Yoo-hoo, Kirby. It's time to come upstairs."

He claps his hands, pretending not to hear. "Let's go," hollers Kirby. "Batter up!"

A few base hits later, his mom's voice booms out again, this time for the entire housing project to hear.

"Kirby Puckett, what did I say? It's getting dark, you get up here this minute!"

The boy winces.

"Hey, Kirby," a friend taunts. "Your mama's calling you."

"Ooh," his teammates join in. "You'll be hurtin' for certain."

A blush of red burns his face. He rushes upstairs. By the time he reaches apartment number 1404, his embarrassment is forgotten. Kirby knows his parents' rules. He can play ball all day long but as soon as night descends, he must come home. He sits out on his apartment balcony and watches a flood of trouble wash over his ball field. Drug dealers pocket dirty cash. Tough guys fight over nothing.

But Kirby feels safe. He has eight brothers and sisters. They all make a fuss over him because he is the baby of the family. His father toils at two jobs to keep them all fed. His mother works hard to keep their house humming with love. She believes in Kirby's dream to one day play in the big leagues.

"Mom," Kirby says. "Everyone says I'm too small. They tell me I look like a fire hydrant."

"Son, there's nothing you can do about how tall you are. All I know is you're never too short to get picked first by your buddies in those choose-up games."

All through junior high school, Kirby is still first pick in sandlot games. Sure, he's a great athlete, but the real reason everyone wants Kirby on their team is his spirit. He loves baseball so much that he never gets tired or discouraged, no matter the score or how blazing the heat of Chicago summers.

He makes his high school team. The playing conditions aren't much better than on the street. The field is bumpy, littered with broken beer bottles. Only after the team cleans up can they begin to play. Kirby burns up the league, but almost no one sees him do it.

"Mom, I want to be a big-league ballplayer. But the neighborhood is so tough, the scouts won't even come to school to see me play."

"Don't you get discouraged," she says. "I believe in you and sooner or later they'll find you. Kirby, you were born to play baseball."

His parents help keep his dream alive. Every Christmas, his dad works overtime just to get him a new bat or glove. Kirby prays all winter for an early spring.

But it looks like springtimes have run out on Kirby Puckett. By the time he graduates from high school, not one scout has come to check him out. Those who have heard of some guy named Puckett dismiss him when they find out he is only five feet, eight inches—too short for the majors.

His dad has passed away and his mom needs money to keep the family together. The ways things are going, he'll never make a living playing baseball. Too short, too scrawny, no power.

Kirby throws his glove in the closet. He takes a job on the assembly line of a Ford Motor plant.

"I guess my playing days are over," he tells his mom. "I need to pitch in at home now."

"Do you still love baseball?" she asks.

"Yes, Mom, more than anything. All I need is an honest shot. I belong out there."

"Yes, you do, son. Your daddy and I knew it from the first time we saw you swing a bat when you were just a tiny boy. If you love something enough, and if you're good at it, you can't give up on your dream."

Kirby finds a way. After a hard day's work, he plays night games in a tough semipro league. One night, a Minnesota Twins scout named Jim Rantz drops by to see his own son play. But someone catches the scout's eagle eye. He witnesses a guy on the other team take over the game. The kid belts a titanic home run, sprays hits all over the ballpark, steals a few bases, and throws out a runner at home.

His name is Kirby Puckett.

It is a sweltering Illinois night. The players are

dragging. Everyone seems to move in slow motion. Everyone except Kirby Puckett. The scout sees him hustling on every play, backing up his teammates, his head and his heart in the game. The scout scribbles excitedly in his notebook, "Little guy who can do everything. Must be seen. Major-league prospect." Hey, wonders the scout, where's this kid been hiding?

⚾ ⚾ ⚾

*"Welcome back to the sixth game of the 1991 World Series here in the Metrodome in Minneapolis. The score is tied in the bottom of the tenth inning but here comes Kirby. The All-Star and team leader has done it all today, on the field and in the clubhouse. Word is before the game, he gave a pep talk to his teammates who have lost three straight to the Atlanta Braves. I don't know what he said but it sure worked. After getting blown out the other night, and one defeat away from losing the World Series, the Twins have come alive tonight led by Mr. Dynamite himself. His over-the-wall catch off a Ron Gant blast is the only reason we're still sitting here."*

Kirby Puckett walks slowly from the Twins dugout to home plate. The Metrodome is rocking now. The crowd noise is deafening. Forty million fans watch the drama unfold on TV sets around the world.

Kirby gives himself the same pep talk he had given his teammates right before the game. They were down in the dumps after losing three straight.

*All eyes follow Kirby's biggest blast.*

One more and it would be all over. Kirby told his teammates what his mother said when he was about to give up on his baseball career. "If you want it bad enough, you'll find a way."

"Jump on board, boys," he had shouted in the clubhouse. "I'm gonna carry us tonight. We're in the World Series. Let's go out and have a good time."

"Let's go get 'em," his teammates had yelled back.

Now as Kirby settles into the batter's box in the bottom of the tenth inning, all the voices disappear into the October night. He is alone with his mom's lifelong message.

Waving his bat, he stares at Braves reliever Charlie Leibrandt. The first pitch is low and away. Ball one.

The next pitch is almost in the same spot, but the umpire pumps his right hand. Strike one.

Leibrandt's next pitch whistles by Kirby's chin. Ball two.

Puckett doesn't know what to expect. Leibrandt's really mixing up his pitches. "Be ready," Puckett tells himself, "be patient."

The left-hander whips his arm forward like he's firing his best fastball. But it's a trick pitch, designed to fool overeager power hitters. The ball floats toward home plate. Kirby cocks his bat. He waits. He swings.

Crack.

The big bang thunders like a bomb bursting in air.

In one split second of silence they all know . . . the catcher, the umpire, the pitcher, the players in both dugouts, and fifty thousand fans rising to their feet. Kirby Puckett has brought them all together with one perfect swing. And as the ball falls at last into the outstretched hands of the hometown crowd, Kirby flashes a little boy's smile.

All the Twins wait for him to arrive home. He crosses the plate into a celebration of open arms. Kirby is as happy as the kid who many seasons ago hit a twilight double across a battered Chicago playground.

And he would remain a happy man years later even when a sudden illness made him nearly blind in one eye. It looked like his career might be over, but he stayed with his team and he did everything he could to play baseball again.

Puckett was swamped with warm wishes from fans, from teammates and even opposing players. They all said baseball needed good guys like Kirby Puckett.

Too short, too scrawny, too poor. Kirby Puckett waves good night to the crowd, leaving every young fan in America with the message he learned from his mother: Yes, you can.

# THE PROMISE

## Mo Vaughn

"Hey, Mo, there's a call for you from Boston."

Mo Vaughn can barely hear above the clatter of cleats and clubhouse chatter. Deep into his rap music, the Red Sox slugger is putting on his road uniform, focusing on the game ahead.

"Whoever it is, tell 'em I'll get back to them after the game," he says.

"Okay, Mo, I'll tell the kid you'll call him later."

Mo Vaughn stops everything. "Wait," he says. "I'll be right there. Tell him to hold on."

Big Mo lumbers across the clubhouse toward the phone. Opposing pitchers might find this 220-pound hulk menacing, but his young fans know better. Mo loves kids.

"Yo, Jason," says Mo. "Thanks for calling. How 'ya feeling tonight?"

He knows the boy calling from a Boston hospital is real sick.

"Yeah, this California team always gives us trouble.

The game's starting soon. Now, listen pal, I want you to keep your chin up. I'll see you as soon as I get back to Boston. . . . What's that, Jason? You want me to hit a home run for you tonight? Whoa, son, I can't promise. . . . Okay, I'll give it a shot. You watch me."

Mo Vaughn hangs up the phone and shakes his head. "I really blew it this time," he whispers. "What was I thinking about, promising a home run? I'm lucky if I get a hit in this ballpark."

Mo's right. Promising a home run against ninety-mile-per-hour fastballs is risky business. He's bound to disappoint Jason.

The thing is, Mo Vaughn would do anything for his young fans. Ever since he was a struggling rookie and the crusty Boston fans booed him all the way back to the minors, the kids always cheered him. They helped him to hang in there. Even after he became a big-league All-Star, Mo never forgot the kids. He was always visiting schools in tough neighborhoods, pumping up the students to keep trying.

When Mo talked, they listened. He spoke the language of hope. When he hung out with sick kids at hospitals, he always made them feel better. That's where he met Jason. They became close. And on this night in California, Big Mo is trying to come through in a big way for his young buddy.

*"Now batting for the Red Sox, number forty-two, Mo Vaughn."*

The slugger grips his bat and marches to the plate.

*Mighty Mo launches a rocket.*

"Come on, pitcher," he thinks to himself. "Give me something to hit. I can take you deep."

Mo swings hard but goes out softly. No home run.

A couple of innings later, Mo digs in again. He grips the bat even tighter.

"Come on, man, do it for the kid, you promised. He's real sick and he's counting on you."

No luck. No home run.

Mo comes up for a third chance. By now, he's kicking himself. "Never should have promised. That was stupid."

"Time!" says the ump.

Mo steps out of the batter's box and takes a breath. "Hey," thinks Mo, "you always tell Jason to keep trying. How can you give up? Get back in there and let it rip."

And when the next pitch zooms in, the big man waves his bat like a magic wand. He connects. In a heartbeat, he sends the fireball flying toward the heavens.

Higher and higher it sails.

Mo closes his eyes, puts his head down, and floats silently around the bases.

Back in Boston, a boy in a hospital has just received his friend's special delivery message. Written in the language of hope, it says, "Keep trying."

# WORKING FOR THE FUN OF IT

## Cal Ripken Jr.

The president of the United States was talking. He said, *Cal Ripken has reminded America all about hard work. About showing up at the job even when you don't feel like it. That's what we're celebrating tonight.*

*Absolutely, Mr. President,* said the television announcer. *This is a tribute to Cal Ripken Jr. and our American work ethic.*

For months, that's all the experts were yakking about. Cal Ripken breaking Lou Gehrig's consecutive-games streak was a story about the work ethic. The sportscasters said it, newspaper headlines screamed it, even the president of the United States declared it.

Every one of them got it wrong. This wasn't about work; it was about playing a game with love. Anyone who was there that historic night of September 6, 1995, knew it.

Seen from the blimp overhead, Camden Yards sparkled like a shiny baseball diamond. The sold-out Baltimore ballyard buzzed with great expectation. It felt like the Fourth of July, New Year's Eve, and Thanksgiving all rolled into one night of magic.

Fifty thousand friends and neighbors were there to witness a moment in baseball history. Thousands of flashbulbs sparkled like a forest of Christmas trees. Millions of fans across the land waited for their American hero.

Then it happened. A thirty-five-year-old, gray-haired man bounded out of the Orioles' dugout like a kid who just heard the three o'clock school bell ring.

"Play ball!" shouted the ump.

The record that Cal Ripken was about to set—2,131 consecutive games played—began long before he arrived in the big leagues. It started with a young boy running home from school on a spring afternoon in Maryland.

Cal would arrive home, say hi to his mom, and then bolt out the door, grabbing his mitt and slinging his favorite bat over his shoulder. He'd race to the ball field and wait alone for the other kids to show.

Cal couldn't stand waiting. He would pick up the hardball, toss it in the air, and line it into center field. As he scampered around the bases he imagined the crowd cheering and the third-base coach sending him home. He'd slide across the plate and call himself "safe!" Cal Ripken had fun playing baseball before the game even began.

"... *And the home of the brave!*"

Now, a quarter century later, the crowd let out a

*Baserunners come barreling in, but Cal keeps flying high.*

roar, waving "We Love Cal" banners. Ripken stood at shortstop as always, smiling and looking forward to the first pitch. Everyone was waiting for the end of the fifth inning, when the game would become official and Ripken would finally break the record. Ripken, though, was concentrating on winning the game.

In the bottom of the fourth, with the Orioles trailing the Angels, Cal walked up to bat. Camden Yards was like a circus. "Cal! Cal! Cal!" they shouted.

Ripken zeroed in on the pitch. He swung. He connected. The ball kept rising over the left fielder's head, sailing into the stands for a home run.

"I don't believe it!" said the announcer.

It seemed like no one else did, either. He had come through, just like he had for every single game in his incredible streak.

When the O's returned to their dugout at the end of the fifth inning, Ripken's achievement was official. He had played in 2,131 consecutive games, breaking Lou Gehrig's record.

He had asked that ceremonies be held after the game. He didn't want to make any speeches while the game was still being played. He loved baseball too much for that. But the Baltimore fans loved him even more.

Here was a guy who always spent hours after each game signing autographs, a hometown kid who was as much a part of Baltimore as crab cakes and the Inner Harbor.

They rose as one and gave him the longest standing ovation in the history of baseball. Ripken's teammates kept pushing him back out onto the field. He tipped his cap, but the crowd would not stop. Finally his love of the game and his gratitude toward his supporters took over.

He began rounding the stadium shaking hands and giving high fives to fans hanging over the outfield wall and reaching out to him. Behind home plate he hugged his wife and kids and shook hands with his brother Billy. He waved to his mom and dad in the stands. Then he insisted the game go on.

The next day sportswriters all over America wrote about Cal Ripken's work ethic, that he'd be back to work at shortstop the next game. They were right. But for Cal Ripken baseball was much more than a job. It was his love.

Ever since he was a kid, he couldn't wait for the next game to begin.

# THE SHARED VISION

## Wardlow and Lucas

HELLO AGAIN, EVERYBODY. *This is Bob Murphy along with Ralph Kiner and Lindsey Nelson, and welcome to New York Mets baseball. Tonight the Mets take on their Eastern Division rivals, the Philadelphia Phillies, here at Shea Stadium in Flushing, New York. . . ."*

Forty miles away in Metuchen, New Jersey, an eight-year-old boy cradles his tiny transistor radio.

"Hey, Donald. Time to go to sleep. I'll be checking in on you in a second."

The boy hears his father's footsteps coming up the stairs. In a flash he turns off the radio and stuffs it under his pillow. The bedroom door swings open.

"Okay, kid. Have a good night, sweet dreams. By the way, any score yet?"

"No, uh—I mean, how would I know?"

"Donald, remember the rule. It's a school night. No radio."

As the door closes, Don Wardlow begins his sweetest dream. He quickly takes the radio out from its hiding place just in time to hear Bob Murphy say, *"And on a steamy August night here in the Big Apple, Tom Seaver winds up and powers a fastball that catches the inside corner of the plate."*

"Strike one!" bellows umpire Augie Donatelli.

"Yeah!" shouts the boy, unable to contain his joy.

"Yeah what?" asks his father from downstairs.

Donald's heart races as he thinks fast. "I said, Yeah, Dad, good night to you, too."

The boy hates fibbing to his father, but listening to the game has become his favorite bedtime story. The pictures the announcers paint with their words, the roll call of the lineups and batting averages, the crack of the bat, and the roar of the crowd when a home run sails over the center-field fence send him on a journey to the world of the ballpark. That's where young Don Wardlow wishes he could be.

❀ ❀ ❀

In another dark bedroom a few towns away, another boy listens to another ball game on his radio. The Yankees' announcing team of Bill White and Phil Rizzuto have eleven-year-old Jim Lucas muffling his laughter in his pillow.

*"Scooter, this situation definitely calls for a nice soft bunt right down the first-base line."*

*"Holy cow, White, there you go thinking like a man-*

*ager again, but these huckleberries today don't know how to bunt. It's a lost art.*

*"Here's the pitch . . . Holy cow! He lays down a beauty, everybody's safe. Listen at that crowd. I told you these kids could bunt. Don't look at me, White."*

Jim Lucas listens to Yankee games every night even though his team has fallen out of the pennant race. He loves listening to White and Rizzuto because he can tell they're good friends sharing their love of baseball. In the sixth inning Lucas falls asleep and dreams he's in the press box at Yankee Stadium announcing the game with them:

"Hey, Lucas, you huckleberry, no way you're still up at this hour. You've got school tomorrow!"

"Come on, Scooter," says Lucas in his dream. "Let me just do the play-by-play for one measly inning. Please?"

When the alarm wakes him the next morning, Jim Lucas rushes to the porch to pick up the newspaper and check the Yankee box score.

⚾ ⚾ ⚾

Two boys in different towns listening to different ball games. But they shared one vision. They both dreamed of becoming major-league radio broadcasters.

Every night they listened to their favorite announcers. Every day they spent hours doing their

41

own imaginary broadcasts. They couldn't wait to strut their stuff on the air.

When students in Wardlow's high school complained about the principal's boring announcements over the PA system, Don had an idea. He went to the office and volunteered to take on the job himself. For the next three years, Wardlow entertained the entire school each day with his jokes and his upbeat stories.

Wardlow went on to Glassboro State College, where he began broadcasting on the school's radio station. Being the rookie sportscaster, Wardlow asked the older guys if they'd team up with him to start a broadcast partnership. One after another, each of them said no.

His last hope was an upperclassman whose sportscasts he had always admired.

"Hey, you're Jim 'Tiny' Lucas," said Wardlow as they passed each other in the studio. "Great show, man. You know, ever since I was a kid listening to the Mets announcers, I've always wanted to be part of a great broadcast team."

"Holy cow, that's amazing," said Lucas. "Me, too. Except I listened to Rizzuto and White."

"Listen," said Wardlow, "are you up for a challenge?"

"Yeah, man, I hear you're pretty good with all those stats. I could really use your help."

The new team of Wardlow and Tiny Lucas was a match made in baseball heaven. They broadcast Glassboro State ball games. Lucas handled the play-by-play. Wardlow, a walking encyclopedia of facts and figures, chimed in with his colorful commentary.

"Looks like he's squared around to bunt, Don."

"I don't think so, Jim. I think he's faking it— he hasn't bunted in his last two hundred forty-eight at bats. Look for him to hit and run."

"Okay, Don. Here comes the pitch, runners moving, it's a ground ball through the hole. The hit-and-run worked like a charm. You must be able to see the future!"

From the first inning of their first game together, Wardlow and Lucas clicked as a team. Even better, they became best friends, talking baseball long after the final out.

After two years of working together, Lucas graduated. The great new broadcast team was no more.

"I'm gonna miss you, man. Stay in touch."

Wardlow tried working with other announcers but it just wasn't the same. "The chemistry's not there," he would tell Lucas during one of their long-distance calls. Soon, Wardlow and Lucas had bills to pay and they both took jobs outside of broadcasting. But they kept their shared vision alive by talking baseball every chance they could.

Then one night in the middle of a phone call they vowed to go for the gold. Scraping up every last dollar they bought tickets to 125 Yankee and Met games! They'd sneak in their little cassette tape recorder, sit high in the upper grandstand, and "broadcast" the games. Then they'd go home and review it all, inning by inning and pitch by pitch, looking for ways to improve the proud team of Don Wardlow and Jim "Tiny" Lucas.

⚾   ⚾   ⚾

Baseball fans in Connecticut know where to find the heart of the game. Under a moonless summer sky, old men sit on their front porches, families speed by on Interstate 84, boys and girls lie awake in their darkened bedrooms. They are all enchanted by two friendly voices echoing through the black August night. "Hello again, everybody, this is Don Wardlow. Tonight the Hardware City Rock Cats take on their cross-state rivals, the New Haven Ravens, in a crucial Eastern League matchup. I'll be bringing you all the action along with Jim 'Tiny' Lucas and Gizmo the Dog."

"Hi, Don. It's always a pleasure to be sitting by your left side. We have a sparkling night for baseball here in New Britain as the emerald outfield shines under the Bee Hive Park lights. For all of you listening at home or on the road, we've got a box seat right behind home plate reserved just for you."

How many fans listening to Wardlow and Lucas paint the perfect picture of the perfect game could imagine how hard they worked together all those years? Few would know the hours and innings Tiny Lucas spent sharpening his play-by-play delivery.

Fewer still would ever guess that his partner and best friend, Don Wardlow, is blind.

# LA FAMILIA DE BEISBOL

## The Alous

Where in the world is the heart of baseball?

Is it in the twilight meadow where an Iowa farmer and his kids play catch after a hard day in the fields?

Is it on the dusty sandlot on the south side of Chicago where teenagers play an extra inning doubleheader with one beat-up hardball and two cracked bats?

Is the heart of baseball under a Canadian Christmas tree where a seven-year-old girl tries on her first mitt, or is it in an Alabama barbershop where old men remember the glory and hallelujah of Negro League battles?

Some will argue that the heart of baseball pounds in the roar of major-league cathedrals in old Tiger Stadium, brand-new Jacobs Field, in Camden Yards, Fenway, and Three Rivers. Others will discover the heart of baseball in the far corners of the globe, in Tokyo, in Taiwan, in Mexico City.

The heart of baseball lives in all these places. But

nowhere does it beat stronger than on a tiny island in the Caribbean that is the home of the Dominican Republic. Dominicans have two great loves: family and baseball.

Dominican families saw their passion for the game as an escape from the daily grind of poverty. Many of the kids became so good that they were signed by major-league teams in the United States. You could build a championship team around these Dominican stars: Juan Marichal, Raul Mondesi, Tony Fernandez. The list goes on and on. But the "First Family" of Dominican baseball is the amazing Alous, and here's their story.

❊ ❊ ❊

Felipe, the oldest, was wise and patient. He was like the coach of his ten brothers and sisters, always looking out for them. He enrolled at the University of Santo Domingo to become a doctor. He enjoyed playing ball and was also a great track star, but his studies always came first. "Sports is just child's play," his mom always told him.

But when his countrymen asked Felipe to represent them in the 1955 Pan American Games in Mexico City, Felipe couldn't say no. He'd run sprints and throw javelin. Then he'd get right back to his schoolwork. Sometimes, life gets in the way of our best plans.

Meanwhile, down in Mexico City, the left fielder for the Dominican baseball team got into a silly fight with a security guard. He was kicked off the team. A game was scheduled for the next day, and the Dominican coach scrambled for a replacement. He needed a good outfielder, and more importantly, someone who would represent his country with honor.

"Get me Felipe Alou," he said.

In his first game the soft-spoken medical student smashed the ball so far that fans might still be looking for it. By the final game, Felipe was batting cleanup. He delivered four hits and helped defeat the American team. The gold medal belonged to the Dominican Republic.

A scout for the major-league San Francisco Giants had seen enough. "We have to sign this guy."

The Giants offered Felipe a grand total of two hundred dollars to sign a major-league contract. Felipe had promised his parents he would finish school. No one who had grown up in the Dominican Republic had ever made it to the big leagues because the country's poverty—and baseball's horrible color barrier—had prevented it.

But now poverty was about to help make a major-league dream come true. The Alou family owed two hundred pesos to the local grocer. If Felipe signed his contract they could pay off their debt and buy groceries. He signed. Using the study habits that had made him a great student in school, Felipe learned to hit professional pitching. Maintaining the dignity found at the heart of his family, he weathered the shabby treatment often aimed at professional African-American and Hispanic ballplayers in the 1950s. Felipe worked and battled his way to the majors in 1958.

"You're a fine young ballplayer," a reporter told him.

"Oh no," said Felipe. "You must be talking about my brother Matty. He's terrific."

Felipe was right on the money. Scouts soon discovered that the Alou boys made great ballplayers. Matty joined Felipe on the Giants in 1960.

"Hey, Matty," said a reporter. "Felipe told us you were the star of the family."

"Oh no," said Matty. "He was talking about our younger brother Jesus."

On September 15, 1963, the Alou brothers made baseball history.

*"Welcome fans. The Giants have taken the field here at Candlestick Park, so let us set the defense for you. In left field, it's Alou; in center field, it's Alou; and over in right field—unbelievable—it's Alou."*

This was the first and only time three brothers had played together in one major-league outfield. The Alous had put a new twist on an old saying. "The family that plays together, stays together."

But as with all brothers, there was plenty of

*Jesus, Matty and Felipe . . . brothers in arms.*

friendly competition. Take the race for the 1966 National League batting title. Matty, now playing for the Pittsburgh Pirates, laid down twenty bunts and beat out thirty infield hits on his way to a .342 average and the batting title. Felipe had 218 base hits that season, more than anyone else in the league, and belted thirty-one homers. But his .327 average wasn't good enough to beat out Matty, his kid brother. Joined by Jesus, who batted a solid .280 over fifteen big-league summers, the Alou boys put together some dynamite numbers. By the time they all retired as players in 1979 they had collected over five thousand hits!

But the Alous weren't done with baseball.

Felipe began managing winter ball in Latin America. Players found that he was a great teacher— patient and wise. He was also fair.

When a veteran player broke the team rules, Felipe fined him. That player was none other than his brother, Jesus. If he's going to fine his own brother, the other players figured, he's going to expect us all to do what's right.

Jesus learned how to be a teacher, too. When one boy in the Dominican Republic proved that he had a world of baseball talent, Jesus took the time to show the boy the fine points of the game.

That boy was Felipe's son, Moises. And, sure enough, the professional scouts soon came calling. You can't go wrong signing an Alou, they agreed.

In 1986 Moises was chosen as the number one

draft pick of the Pittsburgh Pirates. Four years later, he joined the Montreal Expos, a struggling young team. The Expos sorely needed a manager who was wise, patient, and fair.

In 1992 Felipe Alou was given command as manager of the Montreal Expos. He also had the job of managing his son.

"Wonder if he'll play favorites," the young players thought.

They soon found out. One day Moises broke a rule on the team bus. Felipe benched him for the next game. Moises was stung. He and his dad had always been close. His father was his buddy, his hero. Then Moises thought about it and understood. His dad was trying to show the team he would never play favorites on the ball field. Moises responded with a solid, spirited season.

The Montreal community loved and respected Felipe. He took the time to learn French, the language of their city. He showed them that the pulse of baseball beats in every language and in every land.

And the young Expos blossomed under Felipe's leadership. They weren't high-priced stars but they took on their manager's character. They played with such smarts and heart that in 1994 they defied the experts by winning the National League East. The Expos were led by Moises and a young relief pitcher named Mel Rojas—Moises's cousin and, you've got it, another member of the Alou clan.

The family of baseball lives on. On an emerald field somewhere in the Dominican Republic, Moises is teaching two young prospects how to find the heart of baseball. The boys, Felipe and Luis, are his half brothers.

Keep your ears open. Sometime early in the twenty-first century, you'll probably hear an announcer say:

*"In left field, it's Alou. Over in center field, it's Alou. And playing right field—yes, fans—it's another Alou."*

# NEW KID IN TOWN

## Hideo Nomo

You're Hideo Nomo and you're the new kid in town. You don't speak the language, you don't eat the food, you don't know the people. Everything feels strange to you, everything except the baseball in your long right hand.

The Dodgers saw you pitch in your homeland of Japan, where you are called "the Tornado." The scout didn't understand your language, but he understood your fastball. It came whistling toward home plate faster than a Tokyo supertrain.

They asked you to come to America.

You flew across the great Pacific Ocean. Away from your friends, your family, everything you ever knew to be true. You were greeted by people who said you couldn't make it here. They said no Japanese pitcher ever made it big in the major leagues. The players are bigger here. You got nothing to show us.

They'll power you and your fastball back to Japan. And now you stand alone on the green diamond of

Dodger Stadium. You look into the eyes of catcher Mike Piazza. He's been a friend to you, smiling and patting you on the back even when words cannot be understood. He crouches behind home plate, wiggling his index finger under his catcher's mitt. That's the universal signal for a fastball. You got it, no problem.

You go into your big windup. Your leg kicks high, your back swivels to face the batter. Then you whip forward, the baseball suddenly springing from your hand.

The umpire screams something that sounds like "Stee-rike!" His right arm pumps high. You know that sign in any language.

Strike one.

Strike two.

Strike three.

Wait until we see you again, say opposing batters. We'll time your delivery. We'll show you you're just a one-game wonder. You got nothing to show us.

You don't understand a word they're saying. It is only you and your catcher. "Pizza," it sounds like you call him. And every time the two of you connect, he pumps his fist and smiles at you.

⚾ ⚾ ⚾

Soon you're winning big ball games. Now your world's a lot bigger than just you and "Pizza."

Fifty thousand people are telling you something and you get the message. It's the roar of the home-

*In any language Nomo is a winner.*

town Dodger fans. They welcome you every time you come out to pitch. It's music in any language.

The pressure builds. You're a hero back home in Japan. They gather by the thousands in the streets of Tokyo, watching you pitch on big-screen satellite TVs. You don't want to disgrace them. And suddenly, the Dodger fans are expecting you to win every time you pitch.

You look in for the sign from your friend Mike. You've developed a special sign language with him. As you perch on the lonely hill they call the pitcher's mound, Mike is the only one in the world who really understands you.

You go into your long windup and aim right for Pizza's glove. Strike three. Ball game's over.

Baseball writers swell around you in the clubhouse, talking to you through an interpreter. They always knew you'd make it, they say. Your picture is plastered on cover pages of baseball magazines.

You're named the National League's starting pitcher for the 1995 All-Star game in Cleveland. Not bad for a guy who they said couldn't pitch in the major leagues. Now fans across the nation are watching the new kid in town.

The fearsome American League hitters aren't worried. What's the big deal? they wonder. This new kid has nothing to show us.

America remembers that night. They remember how you made the toughest sluggers in baseball swing and miss. But, mostly, the fans remember what you did as you walked to the dugout after your last pitch.

You tipped your cap.

The Cleveland crowd went crazy with delight. You don't understand why.

In that small gesture of grace, you reminded American baseball of its gentle beginnings. There was a time, not that long ago, when most every pitcher tipped his cap to the fans after the game. And fans applauded the pitcher, even if he played for the visiting team. There was also a time not that long ago when players and fans had respect for each other, and both had respect for the game. That's why they're cheering you.

You came to us a stranger.

You excited us with your pitching pizzazz.

You showed us something about ourselves and the game we love.

You're Hideo Nomo, and you're the new kid in town.

# A TALE OF TWO CITY KIDS

## Manny Ramirez

Pop. Pop. Smoke and pop.

The kid threw bullets and he knew it. He blew away the toughest hitters on the block. Even gruff, gray-haired Brooklyn men who had seen 'em all knew that this fireballing Bensonhurst boy was the real deal.

"The paper says the kid's got a tryout with the Mets," said one of the old-timers.

Steve Mandl would hear them talking and picture himself a big-league star. He always dreamed of pitching for the Los Angeles Dodgers, palm trees swaying in the distance. A sold-out stadium would be cheering his every strikeout, his friends and family yelling the loudest. Swing and a miss, strike three, a no-hitter . . . and Steve Mandl would tip his cap to a thunderous hometown ovation.

Steve was proud he was a good ballplayer. As an outsider in a tough neighborhood, it earned him respect. He was an all-star at basketball, too.

One day he was soaring for a rebound and on his way down he heard an awful sound.

Crack.

The kid had hurt himself and he knew it. His knee was smashed to pieces. He knew he couldn't play baseball anymore. At seventeen, Steve Mandl felt like he'd lost his best friend. He bounced around from job to job. He didn't make much money, the work was boring, and his glory days were gone. Life without baseball was life without hope. In time, he went back to school and became a substitute gym teacher at George Washington High School in New York City. He hated it. He didn't know the kids and they didn't know him. He was about to give it up.

Then, one morning, the principal was running around the halls frantically. The school's baseball coach had suddenly quit.

"Do any teachers here know anything about baseball?"

"I do," said Steve Mandl.

"Who are you?" asked the principal.

⚾   ⚾   ⚾

Pop. Pop. Smoke and pop. Twelve-year-old Manny Ramirez heard the gunshots ring out down his block. His new life in America was scary.

Every day the bullets whizzed by. Every night, the drug dealers took over the streets and peddled their poisons. Manny would fall asleep to the screaming lullaby of police sirens and ambulance wails in his Washington Heights neighborhood.

He had come to New York City from the Dominican Republic. And like so many others from his country, Manny dreamed of becoming a big-time ballplayer. The only problem was Manny didn't have a glove, a bat, or a hardball. His parents didn't have the time or the money. He was on his own.

Manny loved baseball and had to find a game any way he could. He played in the crowded streets with a broomstick and a sponge ball. He hit the ball twice as far as the other kids.

He was strong as an ox and he needed to play with the big guys. That meant trouble, because in this neighborhood, some of the big guys were the most feared drug dealers in New York.

When these players took the field, they played each other for big bucks. It was dirty money, earned from selling crack and heroin to young neighborhood kids. Manny stayed away from drugs but he couldn't stay away from baseball. Word got around that the big kid could hit the ball a mile. The drug dealers stuck him into the lineup.

The kid was matched against grown men. When he hit, the gangsters loved him. But once, when Manny struck out with the bases loaded in the bottom of the ninth, he had to run for his life. He was rescued by the neighborhood of baseball. He found out about a youth league in Brooklyn and traveled an hour each way on the rickety subway just to have a chance to play. Back in his own neighborhood, under dim lights, he played long into the night. Maybe Manny Ramirez didn't have a nickel to his name. So maybe he had to live on the meanest of streets. Maybe he couldn't speak the language of his new homeland.

But he understood baseball. And when he dug into the batter's box of a city park, he planted his roots in America.

Meanwhile, Manny's friend, a kid named Roberto, a pitcher for the George Washington High School team, was pleading with his coach.

"You gotta check out my friend, Manny. He's only fourteen, but he's really good."

"Forget it," the coach said. "Bring him around next year when he gets to high school."

"No, please," Roberto said. "Check him out now."

When Steve Mandl, baseball coach of George Washington High School, saw a big kid walking across the field, he figured, "This has to be Ramirez."

"Hey, why not give the kid a shot?" thought Mandl. "Looks like he could use a break." Since becoming a coach, Mandl felt at home with his life again. "It used to be all about me," he'd say. "Now it's all about the kids."

*Working through hard times brings Manny happy returns.*

"Hey, pal," Mandl said to the shy kid. "I hear you can play ball."

Mandl told Ramirez he was too young to play on the high school team, but he'd try him out in a few practice games. He worried that young Manny would be overmatched.

First time up for Ramirez, crack, base hit. Next time up, double. Boom. Triple. Single. Home run. Double again. Over four games, Ramirez went nine for nine.

"Guess you can play some," Mandl said, smiling.

The next year Ramirez was the star of the team. He belted round-trippers over the fence, but he wasn't home free. The streets wouldn't let go of Manny Ramirez. The drug dealers beheld this big strapping kid and they thought he'd make a good bodyguard.

"Yo, kid," they said. "You want to make some easy money?"

"No," said Ramirez, who didn't have a penny in his pocket.

He was a ballplayer. Every morning Ramirez would get up, strap a spare tire to his back, and run twenty blocks to school to build up his muscles. Coach Mandl would smash ground balls to him until the sun went down. Then he'd buy dinner for the hungry third baseman.

Ramirez still couldn't speak English very well. School was hard and he skipped classes. Mandl heard about it and made sure he showed up.

The next couple of years, Ramirez and Mandl were part of a great New York City story. Together, a bunch of poor kids from mean streets and a broken-down ex-prospect who once soured on life created the sweetest of baseball dreams.

And when George Washington won the city championship, Steve Mandl and Manny Ramirez gave each other a bear hug.

Ramirez was the first-round draft choice of the Cleveland Indians, then baseball's sorriest team over the past fifty years. Within a season, Ramirez made it to the big leagues. His first major-league game was at Yankee Stadium, just across the river from Ramirez's old neighborhood. Just about the whole neighborhood was there to see him. Except for his friend, Roberto, the pitcher who had begged Steve Mandl to give Ramirez a shot. The streets had killed Roberto. Years of living on the edge had taken their toll.

When Ramirez took his turn at bat, a roar of desperate hope rang out from his cheering section in the upper deck.

"Manny, Manny, Manny!" they shouted, begging him not to fail.

*Crack.* The ball rocketed deep into the New York City night. The Yankee outfielders raced back and then just watched, along with the world, as the ball sailed over the big black wall. Home run.

Some say you can still hear the cheers in

Washington Heights. You can hear them every time a poor kid swinging a broomstick pretends he's All-Star Manny Ramirez. And you can hear them at George Washington High School, every time Coach Steve Mandl opens another box of baseball cleats donated by Manny Ramirez. These cleats will be running the bases in search of another American dream.

# THE FUNTASTIC
# MR. KRUK

## John Kruk

Why is this guy laughing? Would you be giggling if you looked ridiculous in front of fifty million people? John Kruk is in stitches about it and now he's got the entire country cracking up with him.

Picture this:

It's the 1993 All-Star game, the classic matchup of baseball's best players from both leagues. Fans around the globe watch the quickest, strongest athletes strut their stuff.

There's graceful Junior Griffey of the Mariners gliding across the outfield. Warming up on the sidelines is tall and muscular Fred McGriff from the Atlanta Braves, looking like he's chiseled out of stone. There's Ripken and Ozzie, Gwynn and Carter, looking fit and ready to rock the house.

And then there's John Kruk, who looks like he just ate a house. He's the first to admit he doesn't look like a typical All-Star. He's big and round and scruffy. Fans get on him for looking out of shape, but

*The unsinkable, unmistakable, unlikely fan favorite.*

Kruk doesn't mind. He can hit a baseball as hard as anyone. He made the All-Star team, the same as guys who look like Greek gods.

Kruk was having a ball. He got to meet his favorite players and they got a kick out of hanging out with him. Plus, Kruk couldn't get enough of those All-Star eats. Yep, it's one big party to the fun-loving Mr. Kruk. That is until he actually has to get up to bat in the first inning. Kruk looks out to the mound and sees Godzilla.

He has been dreading this moment ever since he found out the starting pitcher for the American League was Randy Johnson. Kruk had never faced the Big Unit, but he had heard plenty of horror stories about the flamethrower.

The Seattle ace stands nearly seven feet tall. His unshaven face is as scruffy as Kruk's. And as for his hundred-mile-per-hour fastball, well, sometimes Johnson himself doesn't know where it's heading.

The pitcher goes into his big windup, his stringy shoulder-length hair flying. Those long arms seem to stretch halfway to home plate. Out of this hurricane of motion his blazing fastball explodes.

John Kruk sees all this coming at him. Everything except the baseball. It's tough for a lefty hitter to see a ball thrown by a lefty pitcher, especially when Randy Johnson's on the mound. All Kruk hears is a whizzing sound flying over his head.

He ducks, but the ball has already blown by him.

Some All-Stars would be so embarrassed and angry, they'd charge the pitcher. Others might hide their fear by pretending to dig in closer to the plate. Not our John Kruk.

He steps out of the batter's box in front of fifty million viewers, clutches his heart, and wipes his brow in relief. He laughs.

It's such an honest reaction, the fans laugh along. They know it's spooky to face Johnson, especially the first time.

Kruk steps gingerly to the plate. He waits for Johnson's next pitch. Does Randy throw another one of his Godzilla fastballs?

No way. Johnson makes him look silly with a wicked curve. The ball starts out straight for Kruk's head. Our guy ducks. It dances into the catcher's mitt. Strike one. Well, you can probably guess strike two comes in an awful hurry, Kruk waving at it as it floats by.

Kruk knows he's looking goofy, but he can't see the pitch coming. He thinks to himself, "I don't want to get killed on national TV. Dead guys don't hit so good."

By now, the crowd is whooping it up. He steps up bravely. Well, almost. He's standing a taxicab ride away from home plate.

Which is why when the next pitch comes in, Kruk is certain it's going to curve over the plate. He swings. The ball ends up two feet outside.

Strike three. The crowd roars.

Kruk is laughing at himself. He salutes the pitcher, who is grinning innocently like the cat that swallowed the canary. The entire ballpark is hysterical.

"Gee, that was fun," says the announcer.

You bet. That's our John Kruk. Mr. Funtastic!

# THE RIGHT CALL

## Steve Palermo

Cal Ripken rounds third and they're sending him in. Outfielder Devon White uncorks a bullet toward home. It's going to be close.

Ripken slides. The catcher slaps the tag. Out of a cloud of dust rises the right hand of umpire Steve Palermo.

"Yer out!" barks Palermo.

The Orioles manager charges toward Palermo as if launched from a cannon.

"Whaddya mean he was out?" screams the manager. "He was safe by a mile! You must have had your eyes closed!"

Umpire Steve Palermo lets the Os' skipper have his say. He knows the manager wants to win as much as Palermo wants to make the right call.

"He was out, pal," says Palermo softly.

With the crowd booing the ump, the manager screams his lungs out a while longer. Then he trots back to the dugout, defeated. Worse, he knows

Palermo was probably right. The guy's the best umpire in the league.

But the home crowd is letting Palermo have it. A cascade of forty thousand boos falls on him, echoing throughout the old stadium.

Years later, Steve Palermo sits in a chair and remembers. The ump wants to let you in on a secret. He'd give anything to hear those boos again.

⚾ ⚾ ⚾

Like most kids in his Massachusetts hometown, Steve Palermo loved baseball. As much as he enjoyed playing, he liked umpiring even more. He had a passion for the rule book, the split-second calls, the close plays at the plate. At the age of thirteen he worked Little League games. Coaches and parents who had forgotten their manners might holler at the young ump, but Palermo always stuck to his decisions. Even then he could take the heat.

Palermo dreamed of being a big leaguer. He heard about an umpire-training school way down in Florida. He knew he had to go. Most umps, even the ones who graduate from special schools, never make it to the big leagues. The few who do must toil in the minors for ten long years. Steve Palermo was such a phenom that he made it to the big time in almost no time.

What made Steve Palermo so special?

"Being an umpire is about quickness," he says.

"Not running fast but making fast decisions. It's warp speed," Palermo explains. "It's like you have a high-speed camera in your head. You're taking pictures of something that just exploded and you see it all in your head."

And Steve Palermo can still see July 6, 1991. It was a Saturday night. He had worked third base in a game between the Angels and the Rangers. It was hot even when the game ended; Texas summers are like that.

Palermo met some friends in Dallas and they went for a late supper at an Italian restaurant. Palermo loved good Italian food so he ate there every time he was in town. He and his buddies sat at the table, laughing it up, recalling some of the great shouting matches Palermo had waged with half-crazed big-league managers.

"All you worry about is making the call," said Palermo. "If you make the right decision, it doesn't matter what happens after."

At 12:30 A.M. they heard a restaurant worker hollering. Two women who had left the restaurant were being attacked outside.

Palermo made an instant call.

"The five of us were up and off the table," he recalls. "We ran outside to help."

Two of the muggers jumped into a waiting car. A third guy ran away down the street. Palermo and his friends chased him for three-quarters of a mile. They got him. They held him down while someone went to call the police. That's when another one of the muggers came back. He pulled out a gun and fired five shots.

"It was like slow motion," Palermo remembers. "I was aware of everything as it was happening. I heard each shot. I remember each one."

*Bang. Bang. Bang. Bang. Bang.* One bullet slammed into Palermo's spinal cord. He fell. He tried to get up. He couldn't move.

An ambulance took him to the hospital. Saturday turned into Sunday and then Monday. And then Tuesday. And still Palermo was lying in a bed in Parkland Hospital unable to move. A doctor was out in the hall talking with Palermo's wife.

"I knew what he was saying," Palermo says. "He hedged a little, but I remember his words. *You'll never walk again.*"

Palermo was angry. He felt alone. He decided right there he couldn't let the doctor call him out. He was an umpire. He had to walk.

Some people accept a doctor's verdict and give up. "I said, 'Doc, I appreciate your prognosis and I respect you for all the education and experience you have. But I'm going to prove you a liar.'"

Palermo began by wearing braces on his legs. Two months later he was taking baby steps. He had hours upon hours of therapy, until finally he could walk with a cane.

*Umpire Palermo is back at the ballpark.*

In 1991, before a World Series game in Minnesota, Palermo hobbled to the pitcher's mound and threw out the first ball.

Steve Palermo proved to the doctors and the baseball world he could still make the right call. He said he'd walk again and here he was.

The keeper of the rules remains a part of the game. Palermo works in the commissioner's office to make baseball a better game. To make it more fun for millions of fans around the world.

In the meantime, Steve Palermo has made another decision— he would like to be an umpire again.

"It will depend upon my physical ability," he says. "You can't do it if you're forty, fifty, seventy-five percent. I know what it takes. I did it. I know the demands of the job. I know how hard it is."

Right now he is not ready to get behind home plate again and call balls and strikes, to serve as the keeper of baseball's rules.

That hot night in Dallas, four bad guys broke bigger rules. They were hurting people. Palermo couldn't stand by.

"I've had years to play it over and over again in my head," Palermo says. "I have no reservations at all. It was the right call."

# THE LAST ONE PICKED

## Mike Piazza

A poor boy named Vincent Piazza dropped out of high school. Bad move. Chances of a kid like Vincent making it were one in a million.

The boy refused to quit on life. He used the only tool he owned —hard work. Through grit and determination he grew up to become a successful businessman.

"You can't keep a good man down," he'd say. People liked Vince. The guy wouldn't quit.

He had a friend who wouldn't quit, either. His name was Tommy Lasorda. Tommy was a career minor-league ballplayer. His years of hard work landed him the job as manager of the Los Angeles Dodgers.

Lasorda would come over to Piazza's house to visit his five kids. Vince named the youngest one Tommy and asked Lasorda to be his godfather. But the Piazza kid with the big dream of making it to the major leagues was fourteen-year-old Mike.

He was a strong kid. He could hit the ball a mile. Playing for his high school team, Mike destroyed the school home run record held by Andre Thornton, who went on to become a big-league slugger.

No one worked harder than Mike. If the scouts came around he'd be ready. He'd show 'em.

The big-league scouts did show up. They were not impressed. They said Piazza was too slow and that there were thousands of ballplayers better than him.

"Forget it, kid," they said.

And why shouldn't he forget it? His father was rich. Mike was set for life on Easy Street.

But that's not what big-league dreams are all about. That's not what the Piazzas were all about. They believed you couldn't keep a good man down.

Piazza went to the University of Miami, which had one of the country's finest baseball programs. The coaches there had seen better players, too. They sat him on the bench.

The few times Mike did get up, he flopped. He got only one measly hit in nine times at bat. Miami's coaches had no use for him.

Let's stop for a minute. This guy was a bust on his college team and he still thought he had a real shot at the big leagues.

Give us a break.

Mike Piazza still searched for his break. The next year he played ball for a community college. He hit a whopping .364.

Back in Los Angeles, Dodger manager Lasorda heard the good news from Mike's dad. Lasorda begged a Dodger scout to take a look at the young player.

The scouts looked. The first baseman didn't come close to getting a hit. They went back to Lasorda and told him this Piazza kid was no ballplayer.

"Forget it," said one scout's report.

But Tommy Lasorda knew this ballplayer was more than just speed and power. He was Vincent Piazza's kid. Lasorda didn't need to read a scouting report. He knew the Piazza family.

"Please draft him," begged Lasorda. "Squeeze him in on the bottom of your list. Make him the last guy."

And so the Dodgers drafted Mike Piazza in the sixty-second round of the 1988 draft. There were about 2,000 players picked ahead of him. In any draft only the top 150 or so ever make it to the major leagues.

The Dodgers didn't even bother to sign him. They hoped Piazza and Lasorda would just forget the whole thing.

Fat chance.

A couple of months later, Lasorda brought Piazza to the ballpark. He introduced him to Ben Wade, the Dodgers' chief scout.

"Come on," said Lasorda. "Just watch this kid hit."

"All right," mumbled the scout, shaking his head.

Piazza stepped up to the plate in empty Dodger Stadium. This was his last chance.

Mike Piazza's entire dream flew into each and every swing.

*Bam. Boom. Pow.* The kid sent baseballs to the farthest reaches of the gigantic ballpark. Over the fence, into the bleachers, banging off the cheap seats deep in left field.

Ben Wade blinked. He rubbed his eyes.

"So, what do you think?" asked Lasorda.

"He hit 'em where I never seen 'em hit before," said the Dodger scout. "We'll sign him."

"Mike, we'll give you a minor-league contract," Wade told him.

Piazza was bursting with joy.

"Oh, and one more thing, Mike. You're not a first baseman anymore. You're a catcher."

The Dodgers might as well have told Piazza they wanted him to become a duck. Catching is the most difficult position to play in baseball. You need a great arm. You have to be a manager on the field, calling all the pitches the man on the mound must throw. You have to be brave when base runners come barreling into you at home plate. You have to be willing to get scuffed up by foul balls, to dive after sliders in the dirt, to give your legs a daily beating. You need to be the hardest-working player on the field.

"Sure thing," Piazza told them. His major-league dream beat inside his heart. "Let's get started."

*"Error on the catcher, Piazza."*

The scorekeeper for the Dodgers' Salem farm team marked it down on his official scorecard. The fans shook their heads in pity. "Poor kid's no catcher," they thought.

"I'm going to be a catcher," said the young man with the major-league dream.

After his first tough season in the minors, Piazza asked the Dodgers to send him to their winter baseball school in the Dominican Republic. He became the first American player to enroll there.

All winter long, the son of a rich man slaved under foul pop-ups and shots to his catcher's mask. He soaked up the genius of the great Dominican coaches, men who took Piazza under their wings because of his dedication and love of the game.

"Crouch, stand up, now fire to second. Again. Faster. Again. Snap that throw. Again. Better, kid. Now again and again and again."

Back in the minors, Piazza wiped the snickers off the fans' faces. He also wiped opposing runners off the base paths.

"Hey, when did that guy get so good?" everyone wondered.

The Dodgers couldn't believe it, either. This bottom-round draft choice they had signed as a favor

*No one tells Mike Piazza it can't be done.*

to Tommy Lasorda was fast becoming their top catching prospect. In 1992, Piazza sparkled with the Dodgers' top minor-league club, batting a muscular .354 and clobbering twenty-three homers.

He was turning into a fine catcher, too. In September of '92, the Dodgers brought Mike Piazza up to the big leagues. His first game was at Wrigley Field in Chicago.

Piazza came out on the field and looked around at the great old ballpark. He saw the beautiful ivy hanging on the outfield walls. He heard the diehard Chicago fans bellowing "The Star-Spangled Banner" and saw the old men on the rooftops across the street staring down at attention.

Mike Piazza felt goose bumps shiver through him. This was a major-league baseball game and he was catching for the Los Angeles Dodgers. "Keep this dream going," Piazza told himself.

The next day, box scores in newspapers across America told the story of one man's dream come true.

Piazza, catcher. Dodgers.

Three hits in three times at bat.

A perfect day.

The box score couldn't capture the smiles of two proud men—Tommy Lasorda and Vincent Piazza.

"Beginner's luck," muttered all the scouts who had said Mike Piazza wasn't a ballplayer. "He'll cool down. Just wait until he plays every day next season. Yeah, just wait."

In 1993, Mike Piazza enjoyed one of the most incredible rookie seasons in major-league history. He batted .318. He slammed thirty-five home runs. He drove in 112 runs, the most by a rookie since 1930!

And the catcher who everyone laughed at had worked himself into one of the finest receivers in the game. He gunned out fifty-eight base runners—a Dodgers record.

The dreamer had triumphed. Mike Piazza could have snarled at everyone who ever said he couldn't make it. He didn't. He was too busy working to improve his game. In his spare time, he gave baseball clinics to young players with major-league dreams. He visited kids in hospitals who were fighting for their lives.

Hard-nosed Mike Piazza had a soft spot for anyone who kept trying.

"You can do it," Mike Piazza told the kids. "Don't believe anyone who says you can't."

They looked at Mike Piazza and they believed.

# CHUMPS TO CHAMPS

## 1995 Atlanta Braves

They won more games than any other team in the nineties. Twice they went to the World Series and each time they came within a game of winning it all. But by the time the Atlanta Braves got to the '95 World Series, some people called them losers. Choke artists. Chumps.

The Indians will whomp them, Cleveland's rooters said. The Braves are sure to find a way to lose, argued the hecklers. Many fans of baseball had dismissed the Braves as a has-been club. The thunderous Cleveland Indians had become America's hot team.

The players on the Atlanta Braves heard it all. And they said nothing. They didn't need any wise guy's approval. They had each other.

There was "Crime Dog" Fred McGriff, who always rescued ball games in the clutch. A shortstop named Belliard, who played baseball as if it were ballet. A righteous right fielder named Justice. A scrappy second baseman named Lemke. And the new kid at the third-base corner was the all-American boy, Chipper Jones. Fresh from the farm and as strong as an ox, his homers were measured by the acre.

Still, few people thought they could stack up against the muscle-bound Indians, who had eight .300 hitters in their lineup. Led by strong man Albert Belle, who could smash home runs with one hand, they led the league in hitting, home runs, and wins. They had powered their way to one hundred victories with the largest first-place lead in modern baseball history, bombed the Boston Red Sox in three straight games, and then beat the Seattle Mariners in six games to win the American League pennant.

And what did the Atlanta Braves have up their sleeves to stop these tough guys? The long arms of the best pitching staff in baseball.

There was skinny Greg Maddux with the glasses, who looked like the last kid to be picked for a team. He didn't even throw fast.

All Maddux could do was put the ball anywhere he wanted and where the hitters didn't like it. He won nineteen games in the '95 regular season, and lost only two.

There was the little lefty, Tom Glavine, who grew up in chilly Massachusetts playing hockey. He was with the Braves before they were any good, when they used to lose a hundred games a year. But he never complained. He just worked harder until he became one of the best pitchers in baseball. He was the ace of the Braves pitching staff until Maddux came.

Glavine didn't get jealous. He was ecstatic that the Braves had someone who might help them win a championship. But the championship never came. Not even with other fine pitchers, like nice guy John Smoltz, who drove batters nuts with a mean forkball. Or Steve Avery, a hard-throwing lefty, who blew the ball past major-league hitters when he was only nineteen.

But these guys couldn't beat the Toronto Blue Jays or the Minnesota Twins in the '91 or '93 Series. They weren't about to become champions against the mighty Indians.

Especially not with Orel Hershiser taking the mound for Cleveland. He was unbeatable in postseason play, 7–0 in the playoffs stretching back to 1988.

And when the speedy Kenny Lofton stole two bases and a run for the Indians to lead off the first game, the fans said, "Same old postseason Braves. Can't cut it."

But Crime Dog McGriff homered the Braves back into the ball game. Greg Maddux took it from there. He moved the ball up and in. In and out. High and tight. Low and away. The Indians tried to guess where he would throw it next, but Maddux always managed to stay one step ahead of them. He made baseball's best hitting team look foolish, shutting them down on just two hits.

*Champs at last.*

Tom Glavine did the job the next game. He had help from his catcher, Javier Lopez, who homered and picked off Cleveland's Manny Ramirez in a crucial play at first to snuff out a potential Indians threat.

The Braves went to Cleveland with a two-game lead in the Series. But the Indians rarely lost in their home park. Just waiting for the usual Atlanta collapse, Cleveland fans sneered.

The Indians hammered Braves starter John Smoltz, knocking him out of the game early. The Braves fought back, but Cleveland finally won in extra innings. The Indians were back with a vengeance.

All the Braves had to offer in the fourth game was Steve Avery, who was injured much of the year and only had a so-so season.

But the Braves weren't going to get rattled. Amid a raucous, sold-out Jacobs Field crowd, Avery shut down the Indians for five innings as the Braves cruised to victory number three.

One more win and they would at long last be champs of baseball. And they had their ace Greg Maddux, the best pitcher in the league, going for them.

This time the Indians were ready. A defiant Albert Belle, tired of all the outside pitches he was seeing, powered a Maddux breaking ball over the wall in the opposite field. Maddux was long gone before Jim Thome put the game out of reach with a home run for Cleveland.

Even though the Braves still led the Series, 3–2, and they were going home to Atlanta, the Indians were feeling very confident.

"If we beat Glavine tomorrow," said Thome, "we'll win the Series." A frustrated David Justice noticed that the Atlanta crowd was not as loud as the Indians' fans. It was almost as if the Braves' boosters, after coming so close before, were too scared to believe.

It all fell on the shoulders of the lefty, Glavine. Maybe it was fitting for him to take the mound. He was the pitcher who had been through it all with this team.

The Indians all agreed this was the biggest game of their careers. Belle flexed his muscles as he looked out at Glavine. Eddie Murray glared. They did everything but get a hit off the southpaw for five innings. In the sixth, catcher Tony Pena blooped a single to center, but that was all she wrote. The game was still scoreless.

Up came Justice in the Braves' sixth. A fan held up a sign: "Hey, Justice, I hope your bat is as big as your mouth."

With the sweetest of swings, he launched a rocket toward right. The ball climbed high into the Georgia night and didn't come down until it was in the embrace of a happy Braves fan. Home run. Atlanta up, 1–0.

Glavine went out and held the Indians through eight innings. Closer Mark Wohlers shut Cleveland down one, two, three in the ninth and it was all over. Finally the Braves were champs. The entire squad poured onto the field. Maddux and McGriff, Jones and Justice, Grissom and Glavine, the World Series MVP.

The Atlanta Braves were finally accepted as the team of the nineties. At long last, they had a championship flag to prove it.

# THE BIG HEART

## Frank Thomas

Ten-year-old Josh was waiting outside the ballpark for the Big Hurt.

"You really going to ask him for an autograph?" his friend asked. "He looks mean. He'll probably crumple you."

You couldn't blame Josh's friend for being afraid. Frank Thomas, six feet five and 257 pounds, makes big-league pitchers shake with fear. Opposing managers are so scared they prefer to walk him rather than see the Big Hurt crush a baseball five hundred feet. He beats up major league pitching so badly that he has been named the American League's Most Valuable Player two times.

During the game the boys had just seen, the Yankee ace reliever had to face the Big Hurt with the bases loaded. The pitcher got so rattled he plunked Thomas with an inside fastball.

The pitcher looked like he had just seen a ghost. He wasn't as worried about giving up a run as much as he was petrified that an angry Thomas might twist him into a Yankee Stadium pretzel.

The boys had also seen Thomas almost beat himself up after he popped up with runners on base. He slammed his huge bat down so hard, it looked like he might start an earthquake. They heard the crash way up in their grandstand seats.

"I don't think he's too happy today," said the boy's friend, waiting outside the stadium. "Let's get out of here."

Josh tugged at his White Sox cap. "I'm staying," he said. "He's my favorite player and I may never get this close to him again."

The trouble with baseball is that lots of the fans' favorite players won't sign autographs. They say they're too busy. Or they argue that kids' dads sell their autographs at sports collectibles shows.

Kids walk away with their heads down. They stop believing in baseball and its heroes. What would the Big Hurt—annoyed after a bad game—do when a young boy named Josh asks for his autograph?

Let's look into the heart of the Big Hurt.

Frank Thomas's first big hurt wasn't about baseball. It was about a broken heart. When he was young, the big guy had a kid sister named Pamela. Boy, was he crazy about the baby of the family.

Frank loved playing with little Pamela. She'd scoot around the room so fast that Frank would giggle until he lost his breath. Then, when Frank was nine

*Those bats look like toothpicks in the hands of the Big Hurt.*

and Pamela was only two and a half, Pamela stopped scooting. She couldn't even walk anymore.

"Come on, Pamela," said her big brother. "Time for breakfast."

Every time she tried to walk, she fell down. He'd call his mom, who was working at the mill. He'd call his daddy, who was working down near the courthouse.

His parents would have to tell Frank the sad news. Pamela had leukemia.

Many kids live a long time with leukemia, a kind of cancer that attacks the blood cells. Pamela wasn't one of the lucky ones. She died on Thanksgiving Day in 1977.

Frank was crushed. He told his father he was going to grow up to be rich so he could wipe out this deadly disease. "I'm going to be a ballplayer," he promised his dad.

Lots of kids say they're going to be big leaguers. It's a wonderful dream. Josh, the boy waiting outside Yankee Stadium for Frank Thomas's autograph, burns with that major-league dream, too.

You need talent. You need hard work. And you need a little luck.

Young Frank Thomas was blessed with plenty of talent. He was big for his age and could whack the ball a mile. He had eagle eyes that allowed him to swing only at good pitches. Frank worked hard, too. He stopped eating junk food. He had his dad pitch to him every day. He even gave up his spot on the basketball team to concentrate fully on baseball.

The one thing Frank Thomas lacked was luck. He smashed the ball silly in his senior year in high school, batting .472. He led Columbus, Georgia, to its first state title, but when it came time to go for the major-league draft, Frank and his dad waited for a phone call. One thousand four hundred and twenty-three players received calls. Frank didn't get one.

He retreated to his room and cried. How could he ever hope to make enough money to beat leukemia if he wasn't even given a chance to play?

Auburn offered the big guy a college football scholarship. He played a few games but his heart was still in baseball. He walked up to the school's baseball coach and begged for a chance.

Soon pitchers around the Southeastern Conference were hoping Frank Thomas would give them a break. He batted a staggering .385 and led his league in hitting. Thomas figured this would give him a good chance to make the United States Olympic baseball team.

Again the young slugger was overlooked.

Thomas kept pulverizing college pitching. Finally he was drafted by the Chicago White Sox. He destroyed minor-league pitching. In 1990 the White Sox invited him to spring training for a major-league tryout.

Thomas powered homer after homer during the

exhibition season. Strangely, the White Sox sent him back down to the minor leagues.

The Big Hurt was hurting. He took it out on Southern League outfield fences, smacking baseballs all over the tiny parks. No one was going to stop him from becoming a big-league star. He was right. When White Sox fans got a look at him, the entire South Side of Chicago rocked for joy. This was the perfect ballplayer.

Unlike most long ball hitters, Thomas almost never swung at a bad pitch. He hit for a high average as well as power. And what power he showed.

"Here comes the Big Hurt," White Sox broadcaster Hawk Harrelson would announce. Opposing pitchers would feel the pain. In his first four seasons, Thomas clubbed 135 home runs and knocked in more than 450 runs.

Former Yankee skipper Buck Showalter respected Thomas so much, he said he'd consider intentionally walking him with the bases loaded. No other ballplayer inspires such fear in big-league managers.

And no ballplayer is as popular among fans and players as the Big Hurt. He is friendly with everyone and never brags. The only thing Frank Thomas wants to hurt more than a baseball is the disease that killed his sister.

He established the Frank Thomas Charitable Foundation, which gives hundreds of thousands of dollars to help doctors find a cure for this terrible illness.

He said the world can't afford to lose any more of its precious boys and girls.

Frank Thomas can't even stand to disappoint one kid. Of course, the two boys waiting for Frank Thomas outside of Yankee Stadium knew none of this. And as the towering first baseman walked out from the players' gate, Josh's knees began to buckle. A security officer got between the boy and the big-league star.

"Mr. Big Hurt," yelled Josh in a thin voice. "I mean, Mr. Thomas, can I please have your autograph?"

He stuck out a pen and a scorecard. "He doesn't even see you," said his friend.

Then Josh looked up. The biggest man he'd ever seen was looking down at him. It was the Big Hurt. Josh turned to run away.

"Hey, where are you going, son?" asked Frank Thomas. "Change your mind because I had a bad day?"

Josh froze. Frank Thomas gave him his tough-guy stare. Josh was too afraid to move.

Then the Big Hurt flashed a giant smile. He signed Josh's scorecard and then Josh's friend's baseball.

"I told you he was a good guy," said Josh's friend.

"Thanks for asking for my autograph," said Frank Thomas.

Then the boys watched the Big Hurt walk away looking ready to scare the next big-league pitcher who dared to try and sneak a fastball by him.

"Wow!" said Josh. "The Big Hurt looks mean, but he's really a great guy."

Maybe they should start calling Frank Thomas "the Big Heart."

# SERMON ON THE MOUND

## Jim Abbott

Hi, *fans. Welcome to Yankee Stadium. What a matchup we've got for you today. Under a gray autumn sky, Yankee southpaw Jim Abbott tries to keep New York's pennant hopes alive. He's got a tough job ahead of him as he takes on the young and powerful Cleveland Indians. He can't tame the Tribe with just a fastball. Abbott's curveball will have to be sharp as a hook."*

The hook. The neighborhood kids are teasing little Jim Abbott again, and he is mad. So what if he was born with one hand. That didn't mean he had to wear a metal hook on the other. He told his dad he wanted to play baseball just like all the other kids. He threw the horrible silver contraption away.

Then, one hot summer afternoon, Jim's dad came home from work and took his boy out to have a catch. He was going to learn how to play baseball one-handed.

"Put the glove on your right wrist, son," urged Mr. Abbott. "Now, when you throw the ball, quickly

*The big lefty bears down.*

switch the glove to your left hand. I'll throw it back to you. Catch it in your glove and tuck the ball and glove under your right armpit like this. Take the ball out of your glove. Throw it back to me. Good! Now, let's do it all over again."

Jim and his dad practiced for hours every evening until he could catch and throw with ease. The boy was a ballplayer.

*"Now fans, we move to the top of the fifth. Abbott has his curveball hooking sharply over the plate, fooling the Cleveland batters. The Indians have yet to get a hit. But Abbott's not out of trouble yet. With one out, Abbott walked a man . . . and now up comes young slugger Manny Ramirez, who hit two huge homers last night. Abbott's got to go right at him. Here's the pitch. Grounder to short, to second for one, over to first, double play. Abbott gets out of trouble."*

Jim was ready for Little League. But a lot of parents shook their heads.

"No way this one-handed kid can play, let alone pitch. That boy's gonna get himself hurt," they muttered.

The only things that got hurt were the opposing batters' feelings. Abbott struck 'em out with an awesome fastball that made the catcher's mitt pop like a hot firecracker on the Fourth of July.

*"Top of the seventh, and fans, the crowd here at Yankee Stadium is starting to get excited. The big, beefy left-hander has yet to allow the Indians a hit. With each pitch the fans are clapping.*

"Fly ball to center. One out. Here comes slugger Albert Belle. He swings. Ground ball in the hole wide of third. Wade Boggs dives. He snares it, rises to his knees, and fires to first. He's out. Two away.

"Swing and a miss. Swing and a miss. Swing and a miss. The crowd roars as Abbott sets Cleveland down one, two, three again. He's got a no-hitter going through seven innings."

Little League is one thing, sneered some experts. You got to give the kid credit for trying, but he's gonna get hurt when the big boys show up. They'll bunt on him like crazy. He'll never be able to field his position.

One by one, the high school batters bunted. One by one, the one-handed pitcher fielded them and threw them out with the greatest of ease. After a few games, the opposing players wised up and stopped bunting. For Jim Abbott there was nothing to it. He and his dad had practiced fielding bunts ever since he was a little kid.

Young Abbott could hit, too. With a ferocious one-armed swing, Jim would crush the ball to all fields.

Pitching was his true love, though.

By the time Jim was ready for college, his arm had earned respect. Coaches and scouts loved his ninety-four-mile-an-hour fastball. Still, they weren't sure he could make it in big-time college baseball. The University of Michigan believed. By his junior year, most of the so-called college experts finally believed, too. They must have been right because Jim was voted to the All-American Team.

*"Fans, if you just tuned in, stay right where you are. Jim Abbott is two innings away from making baseball history. Abbott knows it. The Indians know it. The crowd knows it and they're on their feet, clapping with every pitch. You can cut the tension with a knife.*

*"Ramirez is up. Swing and a miss. Swing and a miss. Swing and a miss. One away.*

*"Ground ball out. Two gone. Here's Sandy Alomar up to pinch hit. Ground ball to Boggs again, over to Mattingly. Three more outs to a no-hitter."*

In 1988 the world found out about Jim Abbott. He was named the starting pitcher for the United States Olympic team. Sportswriters from hundreds of countries swarmed all over him for interviews. They wanted to take a look at this one-handed wonder. They wanted to ask him about his handicap.

"Wait a minute," said Abbott. "I just want to be judged by my pitching. I don't consider myself as having a handicap."

With the Olympic gold medal on the line, the United States team handed the ball to Jim. He had to face the championship squad from Japan. And, with the whole world watching, Abbott went out and pitched a complete game to lead the United States to a 5–3 victory. That day he became an American hero.

*How about that, baby! Yankee teammates share Jim Abbott's joy.*

But the major-league scouts still had their doubts.

"Don't even think about it. There's no way this guy is going to get the best hitters in baseball out. They'll bunt on him. They'll steal on him. It'll be a sorry sight."

*"What a sight this is. The entire ballpark is on its feet. Kids, tell Mom and Dad to come watch. Call up your friends. Jim Abbott, from Flint, Michigan, the kid they said would never make it, is one out away from a no-hitter.*

*"Here comes the dangerous Carlos Baerga up to bat. Cleveland's young second-sacker is one of baseball's best hitters. The crowd is roaring. Players from both teams are on the top steps of their dugouts. Abbott looks in for the sign from catcher Matt Nokes.*

*"He winds up and fires a vicious slider. Baerga tops a grounder to short. Randy Velarde gobbles it up and whips it to Mattingly at first.*

*"He did it! He did it! Jim Abbott has pitched a no-hitter!"*

Abbott pumps his left hand as his teammates swarm over him and knock him down with hugs.

"How 'bout that, baby!" shouts Abbott.

The crowd erupts in a joyful noise and the celebration goes on and on and on.

Jim Abbott stands tall, tipping his cap to a ballpark of believers.

# HONOR THY FATHER

## Buck Showalter

Buck hung up the telephone and knew this was the moment of truth. He had just gotten a call from his boss. He had heard the words he wanted to hear. The Yankees wanted him back as manager for another two years. This was the only job in the world Buck Showalter had ever wanted. Plus they would pay him a half of a million dollars a year to do it. But . . .

There was just one condition, he was told. He had to fire his hitting coach. Take it or leave it.

No problem, most people would have thought. Do what your boss wants, fire the guy, keep your job. But Buck wasn't most people. He was Bill Showalter's son, and he knew what was right.

⚾ ⚾ ⚾

Something scary was going on in the little town of Century, Florida. Nat knew it. His dad kept it to himself as he called the family to supper. Same time as always. Bill Showalter never allowed anything to disturb the Showalter home. He ran a tight ship. When suppertime was called, you never said, "Wait a minute." Big Bill had survived the blazing battlefields of World War II. He had toughed it out as a fullback for the gritty Pittsburgh Steelers. Now, as principal of Century High, he had to weather an angry storm swirling around him.

Little Nat scurried to the dinner table. He sat down with his three sisters, ready to talk about the day. His dad had always said that members of a family had to take time to share their lives and savor their blessings.

Nat looked forward to this time. His dad might look stern, but he had this way of making everyone laugh. Nat would tell him about his afternoon baseball game and his dad would really listen. Nat loved baseball and he knew where home plate was— at the head of the table in the person of Bill Showalter.

But this night at the dinner table was different. Nat could hear his mom and dad talking about something serious. The teachers at his dad's high school had walked out, on strike. They wanted the community to make the schools better. As principal, Nat's dad was supposed to defy the teachers. The problem was, Bill Showalter felt loyal to them. He believed his teachers were right in what they were doing. Nat didn't understand all the grown-up talk, but he already knew what his dad was going to do. If there was something more sturdy than Bill Showalter's six-foot-two-inch frame, it was his rock-solid values.

- You treat everyone fairly.
- You bring passion to your work.
- You are loyal to your friends, your family, and the people who work for you.

Most of all, you have to be loyal to your beliefs. A million people telling you otherwise cannot shake you from doing the right thing.

Nat's hunch was right. His dad would walk out with the teachers. He stuck by the teachers and Nat stuck by his dad. The townspeople were furious. The school board swore Nat's dad would never work again. But then they decided to offer him a job that nobody wanted: to be principal of a school that had to be desegregated.

In 1968 many schools in the South were segregated. This meant that white children and black children could not go to school together. The courts finally ordered schools to be desegregated. That was fine with Bill Showalter, who thought separating kids by race was about the dumbest thing in the world. But the court decision didn't go over well with some white people in Century. They made mean, threatening phone calls to his home late at night. Nat saw that it didn't shake his dad, so he didn't let it rattle him.

Bill Showalter made his son Nat the first white student in the school. Nat made a lot of friends there. All of the kids played baseball together after school, and Nat's dad would come over and watch. As seasons passed, Nat became a great high school ballplayer. He was so good that when it came time to go to college, he got a scholarship to Mississippi State. Coaches loved him, not just because he could hit the ball, but because he played so hard and so smart.

Sometimes another hardworking guy would come watch him play. Bill Showalter would drive three hundred miles in his 1969 Ford pickup and park the truck way beyond right field. After the game, he'd wave to his son and head home.

No lectures about how Nat should play the game. He didn't want to pressure his son. He just wanted Nat to know that his dad was always there for him.

And then a little luck came around for this principal's son from the tiny town in Florida. He was drafted by the New York Yankees. Amazing. When Nat was a kid, he used to watch *The Game of the Week* on television. The first time he saw Mickey Mantle swing a bat, he became a Yankee fan forever.

Nat asked his dad if he was proud of him. His dad smiled and said, "I'm always proud of my children."

Nat joined a Yanks farm team. He got a nickname there— they called him "Buck." It's a name given to tough, scrappy ballplayers. But Buck learned that he was no Mickey Mantle. He couldn't run as fast, throw as far, hit as hard. He still figured he could be the Yankees' first baseman someday.

One day he was playing ball for the Yankees' minor-league team in Oneonta, New York, when a hawk-eyed kid from Indiana joined the team. This young guy had these quick wrists that sent the ball jumping off his bat. He was acrobatic in the field. Yep. Buck saw Don Mattingly and he knew he was looking at the Yankees' future first baseman.

Buck admired Mattingly. They came from the

*Buck and Bill Showalter, the manager and his mentor.*

same tribe of hard workers. It's just that hard work alone wasn't going to be enough to make Buck a major leaguer.

That didn't stop Buck from trying. And it didn't stop him from learning everything he could about the game from his seat on the bench. He couldn't sulk. He loved baseball too much.

The Yankees saw something special in Buck Showalter. He brought passion to his work. He was unshakable. He was loyal to his team even when he wasn't in the starting lineup. Those are the values the Yanks wanted to pass on to their young players. They asked Buck if he wanted to manage one of their minor-league teams.

He was a natural—demanding, but encouraging and patient. When Buck led the Albany Yankees to an incredible one-hundred-win season, he gathered the players around after the last game.

"You did something really special this year," he said. "We may never all be together again. So take this time to enjoy what you've done together. It's important to count your blessings."

Word got around. The Yanks asked Showalter to join the big team as a coach. Manager Billy Martin believed Showalter would one day lead the team. He wanted to teach him everything he knew.

In 1991 the Yanks were looking for a new manager. The people who really knew the game—the players—all asked for one man.

"The guy they should hire is Buck Showalter," said the Yankee first baseman, an All-Star by the name of Don Mattingly.

The Yanks took their players' advice. The day he was hired, TV cameras invaded the Yankee clubhouse. Buck broke away from the mob and picked up his daughter, Allie. He carried her out to the deserted stadium infield, where Mickey Mantle hit the mammoth home runs that Buck watched on TV as a kid. This was a place of tradition. Holding Allie, he thought of his father. Big Bill Showalter wasn't feeling too well. He couldn't be at the stadium with Buck. But Buck could feel his father's presence. Bill Showalter taught his son all he needed to know about life.

Three weeks later his dad died. Only his father's lessons remained. Buck would have to take it from there.

    ⚾   ⚾   ⚾

He built his team day by day, player by player. The Yankees began to resemble their manager. They weren't the most talented guys in the league, but were solid and hardworking and smart. The team was loose and relaxed until game time, but Buck made sure they were always prepared and focused and ready to play their hearts out.

"Time to punch the clock," Yankee captain

Mattingly would yell before the team took the field for each game. The Yanks simply outworked other teams, and in 1994, it all came together for "Buck's Bombers." They had the best record in baseball into August and they were the favorites to win the World Series. But a players' strike loomed. Baseball had grown grumpy. Even after an occasional Yankee loss, the media would attack the manager as if the whole world were crumbling.

"Hey, Buck. How come you didn't pinch-hit for Kelly?"

"Hey, Buck. Why'd you let Key pitch into the eighth inning?"

"Hey, Buck. Are the Yanks choking?"

Microphones and TV cameras were poked at his face. Standing in the center of the Yankee clubhouse, the young manager answered each question politely. Finally he said, "Thanks for your time, folks; we'll be back tomorrow."

He turned to leave, but his office phone rang. It was Buck's boss, George Steinbrenner, owner of the New York Yankees. Buck listened as Steinbrenner went ballistic about the loss. The Yankee skipper bit his lip. He had heard this tantrum before. "Thanks for your call, Mr. Steinbrenner."

"It's a good thing the Yanks are in first place by ten games," Buck thought to himself as he hurried to his car. He battled the big-city traffic until he crossed the river into the green pastures of the suburbs. Buck took a deep breath. "It's nice to be away from that craziness for a while. Why does everyone have to point fingers after a loss? It'll be good to get back home."

Suddenly as he was driving along, Buck saw something out of the corner of his eye. It was a Little League game. Buck pulled off the road to watch. "Now here's what baseball is all about," he thought. He decided to take a seat in the bleachers. Out of his Yankee pinstripes no one recognized him.

"Hey, Jimmy!" screamed a father in the stands. "Bear down —you looked like a jerk your first three times up! That's not how I taught you to hit."

"You're useless, Ump! I'm gonna get you kicked out of the league," came a voice from the third-base line.

"Listen, kid!" screamed the ump. "You don't get into the batter's box until I say so. Do it again, and you're out of the game!"

Buck took it all in and shook his head. This wasn't the way he remembered baseball. This wasn't the way it was when he was a boy.

Buck went home to his family. Each day he was home he'd take the phone off the hook and share a meal with them. "Time to listen to my family," he'd say, "time to count my blessings."

⚾  ⚾  ⚾

When the 1995 season rolled around, everyone expected the Yanks to keep rolling. But three of the

Yankees' star pitchers got injured, including their ace, Jimmy Key. Aging Don Mattingly, his back aching, could not hit the ball with power.

The team stumbled. Fans panicked and George Steinbrenner began ranting and raving. He wanted Buck to bench Mattingly.

Buck remained calm. He said, "Mattingly will continue to play. Don's still a great fielder," he said. "He's the team leader. He shows the other players how to play hard and win. He's earned my loyalty."

Buck was right. The Yanks caught fire in September, winning twenty-six out of thirty-one games. They were led by quiet Bernie Williams, a shy young man brought along by Showalter and hitting coach Rick Down. Captain Don Mattingly delivered key hits and saved games with his dazzling fielding plays at first base.

On the last day of the season, the Yanks needed just one more victory to earn a place in the playoffs. Buck put his trust in a rookie pitcher.

"Buck doesn't know what he's doing," fumed Steinbrenner.

The young pitcher went out and won the game. Buck just watched his players celebrate. He didn't interfere. "It's their victory," he said. "They need time to savor good times."

"The manager's a genius," said Steinbrenner. "I've always said so."

The Yanks went on to play the Seattle Mariners

in the playoffs. It was an exciting series, full of Ken Griffey Jr. home runs, clutch hits by Don Mattingly, and thrilling extra-inning games.

In the end, the Yankees lost. Buck and the players took it hard, but they knew they had tried their best. They tipped their caps to the Mariners, who played just a little better.

"Are you still proud of your ball club?" the reporters asked Showalter.

"I'm always proud of my players," he said. "We'll get 'em next year."

But Yankee owner George Steinbrenner threw another temper tantrum, like the angry father Buck saw at the Little League game. Steinbrenner blamed the loss on the umpires. He blamed it on Buck. He blamed it on the Yankees' hitting coach.

"Buck doesn't know what he's doing," said Steinbrenner. "I've always said so."

Steinbrenner knew he couldn't fire Buck. The Yankee skipper was too popular with the Yankee fans and players, too well respected by baseball people. So he hatched a plot to force Buck to quit.

"Buck, we've got to find a new hitting coach!" yelled Steinbrenner. "If you don't fire your guy, you're gone, too."

Buck thought about his dad. He couldn't be Bill Showalter's son and sell out. "I had to be able to look people in the eye," he said. "I had to look myself in the mirror."

Buck told George Steinbrenner he would not fire his assistant. That was it. Buck was no longer the Yankees' manager. He had lost the one job he had always wanted, but he still had his father's rock-solid values and courage.

Other teams treasured those gifts of decency, loyalty, and passion. Buck was flooded with job offers and took one out west. He would become the head of a new baseball family called the Arizona Diamondbacks. Buck brought with him all his baseball knowledge and experience. He also brought along his entire coaching staff. Most important, he carried with him the proud legacy of Bill Showalter.

# OUR GAME

## Ken Griffey Jr.

It's the All-Star Home Run Derby. The big sluggers of each league have one job—to make the ball disappear over the outfield wall.

One by one, baseball's brutes take their mighty cuts—Cecil Fielder, Barry Bonds, Frank Thomas. With serious eyes they stare down the meatball pitches and swing furiously for the fences. They huff and they puff and they pop it up to second base. They shake their heads in frustration and slink back to the dugouts.

And then a murmur from the fans grows into a rumble and swells to a roar. Ken Griffey Jr. bops up to home plate, dragging the bat, screwing his hat around backward. He flashes a grin that has won the hearts of young America.

The ball comes in. *Whomp*. The ball goes out.

The pitcher throws again. Griffey glides his right foot forward, whips his bat in a lightning blur, and flicks his wrist.

The black bat rockets the white ball into a violet sky. He homers again on the next pitch. Fourteen times. Ken Griffey Jr. not only makes baseball easy, he makes it smile.

Great baseball stories start with a round ball and a wide smile. Playing catch with his big-league dad, Ken Griffey Sr., was always just plain fun. Senior throws to Junior, who leaps and misses, falling to the ground laughing. Junior throws a rainbow back to Senior, and they are at once and forever connected to our national pastime.

Little League was a blast and high school ball was a barrel of laughs. Ken Griffey Jr. was so good at this game that the Seattle Mariners signed him to a minor-league contract at the age of seventeen.

Griffey was still playing a boy's game but pro ball was a man's business, even in the minors. Every swing was judged, every at bat meant so much. Where was the fun? Even his dad got on his case as he slumped miserably. He was homesick and he wanted to quit playing ball. He called his dad and told him how he felt. His dad remembered playing catch in their Cincinnati backyard and he knew what to say.

"Son, this is only a game. Just go out and have a good time."

Dad's words were like a can of spinach to Popeye. Junior busted out of his slump and by his next birthday, he was playing with the Seattle Mariners. He clobbered big-league pitching.

One night at Yankee Stadium he made an incredible leaping catch that had even Yankee fans applauding. No one cheered louder than a proud man in the stands—Ken Griffey Sr.

What amazed fans most about Griffey was that he seemed to be enjoying himself. Baseball had become a grim business and this guy couldn't stop smiling. He couldn't stop hitting, either.

Big deal, sneered baseball's critics. The kid's laughing now, but wait until next year. They'll wipe that grin off his face. He'll start snarling at kids who ask for autographs, he'll throw temper tantrums and demand to be traded.

The critics were wrong. Junior treated baseball for what it was —a kid's game. "He always seemed to be having more fun than the rest of us," White Sox slugger Frank Thomas told a reporter. In 1994, Griffey challenged Roger Maris's single-season home run record. When Maris set the record in 1961, he was so tense that his hair started falling out. Griffey just bopped around like a kid without a care in the world. Fans from every team cheered him on.

And then the unthinkable happened: the Scrooges of baseball beat back joy and the major-league game went on strike. The fans were furious. They missed the pennant races. They missed the World Series. And, most of all, they missed Ken Griffey Jr.'s smile lighting up summer nights.

When baseball came back the next year, the fans

*A flick of the wrist, a crack of the bat, another homer for Junior.*

stayed away. What little enthusiasm there was grew out of the playful heroics of Ken Griffey Jr., who missed most of the season when he broke his wrist while making a spectacular catch.

Baseball tried most everything to get the fans back. They had silly giveaways and they even forced unsmiling ballplayers to mingle with fans.

The men of baseball missed the point: where was the fun? The answer was right under their noses.

It's in the laughter of every seven-year-old child chasing a ball thrown by his father. And it's in Ken Griffey Jr., who kept the smile of a backyard catch and flashes it each time he sends another ball over another major-league wall.

There he was, at last, coming back from the broken wrist to lead the Mariners into the American League playoffs. Smashing six homers and then in the final game, rounding third, risking everything to score the winning run of the series. He tore for home, trying to beat the outfielder's throw. The catcher reached for the ball. Griffey flew through the air and slid into a cloud of dust. Safe! Mariners win.

Happy teammates poured out from all directions, piling on Griffey. And under this mountain of Mariners shines the game's brightest star.

Ken Griffey Jr. plays like you play, he knows what you know—this game belongs to you.

# A NOTE ON
# THE STORIES

We hope you enjoyed our stories. If you have any comments or questions, we would love to hear from you. Write to us at *The Good Guys of Baseball*, c/o Simon & Schuster Books for Young Readers, 1230 Avenue of the Americas, New York, N.Y. 10020.

Someday we bet we'll be reading a book you wrote. We'd like to give you an idea of how we wrote this one.

First, we needed to find out who the good guys of baseball were. Terry Egan, a sportswriter for *The Dallas Morning News*, had interviewed many of these players, Cal Ripken and Jim Abbott, just to name two. Mike Levine knew about Joe Ausanio's story because he wrote for Joe's hometown newspaper, *The Times Herald-Record* in upstate New York. Stan Friedmann asked many young fans which big leaguers they thought were good guys. Between the three of us, we are dads to eleven children, so we asked them, too. Next, we got busy learning all about these special people. Buck Showalter, Steve Palermo, and Joe Ausanio were especially generous with their time. Don Wardlow and Jim Lucas invited us into the announcing booth to watch them work. We also talked with people who knew the players, like Steve Mandl, Manny Ramirez's high school coach.

But even with all these great sources we really couldn't have written this book without the help of our public libraries. Librarians are a gold mine of information. They steered us to books by and about the different ballplayers. We really enjoyed Kirby Puckett's autobiography. Reference librarians showed us how to do research on computers where we found hundreds of newspaper and magazine articles about the players. Wonderful stories from periodicals like *Sports Illustrated*, *The New York Times*, and *The Sporting News* gave us valuable information, as well.

We thought doing research would be a chore. It turned out to be an exciting adventure. If you're interested in finding out more about a ballplayer or a team, go straight to your public library, school library, or local bookstore.

Happy reading!

# SUGGESTED READING

Arnold, Eric. *A Day in the Life of a Baseball Player: Mo Vaughn.* New York: Scholastic Books, 1996.

Aylesworth, Thomas G. *The Kids' World Almanac of Baseball.* Introduction by Cal Ripken, Jr. Mahwah, NJ: Almanac Books, 1996.

Berkow, Ira. *Hank Greenberg, Hall of Fame Slugger.* Philadelphia: The Jewish Publication Society, 1991.

Bernotas, Bob. *Nothing to Prove: The Jim Abbott Story.* New York: Kodansha International, 1995.

Egan, Terry, Stan Friedmann, and Mike Levine. *The Macmillan Book of Baseball Stories.* New York: Simon & Schuster Books for Young Readers, 1992. (Paperback edition published Winter 1997 as *Heroes of the Game: True Baseball Stories*, New York: Aladdin Paperbacks, an imprint of Simon & Schuster.)

Mackay, Claire. *Touching All the Bases.* Buffalo, NY: Firefly Books, 1994.

Macy, Sue. *A Whole New Ball Game: The Story of the All-American Girls Professional Baseball League.* New York: Puffin Books, 1993.

McKissack, Patricia C., and Frederick McKissack, Jr. *Black Diamond: The Story of the Negro Baseball Leagues*. New York: Scholastic Books, 1994.

Puckett, Kirby. *I Love This Game*. New York: Harper Paperbacks, 1993.

Ripken, Cal. *Count Me In*. Dallas: Taylor Publishing, 1995.

Robinson, Ray. *Iron Horse: Lou Gehrig In His Time*. New York: Harper Perennial, 1991.

Rodman, Edmon J. *Nomo*. Los Angeles: Lowell House Juvenile, 1996.

Sullivan, George. *All About Baseball*. New York: G.P. Putnam's Sons, 1989.

Ward, Geoffrey C. and Ken Burns with Paul Robert Walker. *Who Invented the Game?* New York: Alfred A. Knopf, 1994.

White, Ellen Emerson. *Jim Abbott, Against All Odds*. New York: Scholastic Books, 1990.

For more information about baseball, also check out *Sports Illustrated For Kids* and your local newspaper. Ask your teacher or school librarian about the "Newspaper In Education" program.

# PHOTO CREDITS

Page 82, Mike Piazza, circa 1994: *photo courtesy of The National Baseball Library & Archive, Cooperstown, NY/The Sports Group.*

Page 88, Mark Wohlers, October 28, 1995: *photo courtesy of Joe Sebo.*

Page 94, Frank Thomas, March 24, 1992: *photo courtesy of PF Sports Images.*

Page 101, Jim Abbott, August 30, 1995: *photo courtesy of PF Sports Images.*

Page 105, Jim Abbott, September 4, 1993: *photo courtesy of PF Sports Images.*

Page 111, Buck and Bill Showalter (undated): *photo courtesy of Buck Showalter.*

Page 122, Ken Griffey Jr., April 24, 1994: *photo courtesy of PF Sports Images.*

# Don't miss these other great baseball titles from Aladdin Paperbacks!

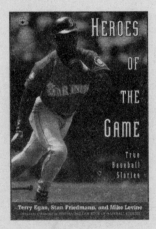

*Heroes of the Game:*
*True Baseball Stories*
by Terry Egan, Stan Friedman, and
Mike Levine
(0-689-81352-X $4.50 US, $5.99 CAN)
True stories about the successes and
trials of major stars, average players,
and even baseball fans.

*How to Snag Major League*
*Baseballs: More Than 100 Tested*
*Tricks That Really Work*
by Zack Hample
(0-689-82331-2 $3.99 US, $5.50 CAN)
Learn how to bring home
the ultimate souvenir from a game
by someone who ought to know—
he's snagged over 1,000
major league balls!

Aladdin Paperbacks
Simon & Schuster Children's Publishing
www.SimonSaysKids.com

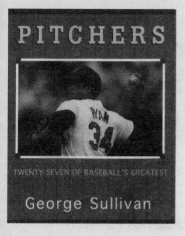

*Pitchers* by George Sullivan
(0-689-82454-8 $7.99 US, $11.50 CAN)
Read about twenty-seven
of the most famous
pitchers in the history
of baseball.

*Sluggers* by George Sullivan
(0-689-82455-6 $7.99 US, $11.50 CAN)
A look at twenty-seven
famous sluggers who have
brought excitement
to the game.

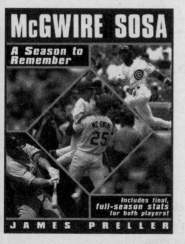

*McGwire & Sosa:
A Season to Remember*
by James Preller
(0-689-82871-3 $5.99 US, $8.50 CAN)
Read about the magical
season of '98, when Sammy
and Mac became a part of
baseball history.

Follow the  on their quest

for the championship in the action-packed

baseball series from Aladdin Paperbacks.

All titles $3.99 US / $5.50 CAN

**Aladdin Paperbacks**
**Simon & Schuster Children's Publishing**
**www.SimonSaysKids.com**